Graded Practice
in Summary
and Directed Writing

Roy Dyche

Longman

LONGMAN GROUP UK LIMITED
Longman House,
Burnt Mill, Harlow, Essex CM20 2JE, England
and Associated Companies throughout the world.

First published 1985
Third impression 1988

Set in 11/12pt Plantin

Produced by Longman Group (FE) Limited
Printed in Hong Kong

ISBN 0-582-33183-8

For Justen and Samantha

Contents

Introduction

Since all the exercises in this book require the writing of some form of summary, you should study the following section of the introduction whether or not you are mainly concerned with the exercises headed *Summary*.

How to write a summary

1 Understanding the passage
Naturally you cannot hope to write a satisfactory summary of something you have not properly understood. Some of the passages included here, especially the later ones, demand close, thoughtful reading and re-reading before you can feel confident of their meaning. Most of them, however, are not at all difficult and will be immediately understood. Even so, it would be wise to read the passage a second time to make yourself really familar with the material. You need to feel you have grasped not only the meaning of individual sentences but also the overall structure of the passage, how each part relates to the rest.

2 Understanding the instructions
Think carefully now about the question you are to answer; you must be quite clear what information it is you are being asked to extract from the passage. The instructions may identify the lines containing the material you need; but you cannot simply assume that the question requires you to summarise *everything* in those lines. Later exercises do not direct you to specific lines and then you must search the entire passage for your material; probably whole paragraphs will be irrelevant to your summary, and certainly you must not expect to find your information neatly packaged in one place. Obviously, then, it is important you understand precisely what you are looking for.

3 Preparatory notes

Now go through the passage — or at least those lines speci-
fied in the instructions — compiling, under suitable headings
if your summary is to be in more than one part, a list of
points you consider ought to be included. At this stage it is
not your aim to express yourself in well-formed sentences,
but it is vital that your notes be thorough and accurate since
you will not be returning to the passage until after your first
attempt at the summary. You should realise:

a It is always expected that the summary will be largely in
  your own words, and it is now that you should try to move
  away from the wording of the original. There will be terms
  and phrases you can hardly avoid taking from the passage,
  but if you can rephrase the material without going to ridiculous lengths, you should do so. *A summary is never
  merely a string of quotations from the passage.*

b Producing a summary is, above all, a matter of grasping
  and then expressing in a clear, economical way the *essential
  meaning* of a piece of writing. Therefore:

  • You must be able to distinguish the main ideas in the
    passage from whatever has been included merely to sup-
    port those ideas and which therefore ought not to be
    summarised. For instance, as a general rule you should
    ignore material the author provides simply to *illustrate*
    his points. You will see, then, that a summary of this
    paragraph would discount everything after the first
    sentence.

  • To ensure he is correctly understood, an author may
    repeat a point, presenting it in a rather different way.
    A careless reader may be led to think separate points are
    being made and, as a result, include two items rather
    than one in his summary. This is a common mistake and
    you should guard against it.

  • To arrive at the essential meaning of a passage, you
    must be prepared to dispense with much of the detail
    and to distil from it the general idea the author intends.
    For example, nothing of importance would be lost from
    the paragraph above entitled *Understanding the instruc-
    tions* if it were summarised: 'Not everything in a passage
    will be relevant to your summary, so you should study
    the instructions until you are quite sure what infor-
    mation you are being asked to extract.' Similarly, a de-

tailed list of related items may often be satisfactorily rendered by a single word or phrase; for instance, you should have little difficulty finding a short expression to summarise the italicised list in this sentence: 'Residents complain that the area has no *swimming-pool, tennis courts or other sporting facilities; neither are there any clubs, cinemas or discos.*' You must take care, however, not to exclude so much detail from a passage that you succeed in saying practically nothing at all!

c Students often distort the sense of the original by treating minor points at greater length than major ones. It is a good idea, therefore, to indicate in your notes the relative importance of points, perhaps by starring those which are emphasised in the passage.

d Of course, your intention is to note *all* the material your answer requires. If you are doubtful about the relevance of a point, add it to the list with a question mark against it.

Before moving on to stage 4, review your notes, making final decisions about relevance, grouping points which clearly ought to be treated together and ordering your material so that, as far as possible, one point seems to lead naturally to the next. Certainly the order information was presented in the passage may not be the best one for your summary.

4 The first draft

Your task now is to turn your notes into a piece of English which, besides being grammatical and correctly spelt and punctuated and, of course, displaying some variety in the sentence structures used, has these qualities:

Plainness

Summary-writing is definitely not a literary exercise and strikingly original turns of phrase, witty similes and metaphors and so forth would be out of place. Straightforward clarity and accuracy are all that are called for on this occasion.

Formality

You should write in a relatively formal way, avoiding shortened forms (*it's, weren't,* etc) and colloquialisms (*lots of, pretty good, big-headed,* etc).

Coherence and continuity
A disjointed collection of isolated points would be a poor summary. You have already tried to order your material so that it develops a single line of thought and should now attempt to make the logic of this arrangement clear to the reader by the use of expressions designed to show the relationship between ideas: *First, . . . Secondly, . . . Finally, however, nevertheless, therefore, moreover, furthermore, as a result* and so on. You will also want to ensure that your first sentence gives some indication of what is to follow; normally all that is required here is some reference to the subject of your summary in the course of making your opening point, for example: 'One important reason for the recent decline in cinema attendances is . . .'.

Conciseness
Wordiness — employing half-a-dozen words when one or two would do the job just as well, padding out a piece of writing with words that serve no obvious purpose, repeating or elaborating points already clearly made — is rarely excusable in any type of writing, but tight, concise expression is particularly important in summaries, which are, by their very nature, exercises in the economical use of language. A word of warning, however: the desire for conciseness should not lead you to produce a summary the meaning of which is obscure or the style of which is 'telegraphic' and inelegant.

5 The final version
You will certainly be able to improve on your first attempt. First check that you are within the permitted number of words. A few words over can usually be easily corrected by more economical wording. If you have greatly exceeded the limit, it is probable you have included irrelevant material and must decide what needs to be omitted. To have used considerably fewer words than were available to you is not normally a matter for self-congratulation: it suggests either that you have expressed yourself too tersely or that you must search the passage for material you have overlooked.

You should now return to the passage, comparing those parts you have summarised with what you have written and asking yourself whether the original meaning would be clearly and accurately conveyed to someone reading only your version.

Finally, having assured yourself that your summary is written in a way that satisfies the requirements set out in stage 4, make a neat copy, crossing through earlier stages when you have finished and stating in brackets at the end the number of words you have used.

The directed writing exercises

Since these too are exercises in summary-writing, most of the advice offered above will hold good: you should adopt a similar five-stage approach, try to use your own words, avoid examples, be concise and so forth. However, not everything said in the first half of the introduction, especially in stage 4, will apply, as we shall see.

Of course, the difference between straight summaries and the directed writing exercises lies in how you are to present the summarised material. The instructions define situations in which you should imagine yourself writing — *real* situations in the sense that they could be encountered in the 'real world' outside the classroom: you might be asked to present your summary in the form of a letter to a newspaper which has recently published an article with which you disagree, or to imagine you witnessed an accident described in the passage and the police have asked you to provide a written statement summarising what you saw.

Although you may feel that writing tasks of this sort are more useful and interesting than conventional summaries, the demands directed writing exercises make on your language skills are generally greater. Unfortunately there is no easy way of preparing yourself for this work. How well you do will largely depend on how aware your English lessons and your own reading have made you of the need for language, if it is to be effective, to be used differently on different occasions.

The most that can be done here is to draw your attention to the considerations you must bear in mind when selecting and presenting your material in answer to questions of this type. In describing the writing situation, the instructions will provide you with all or most of the following information:

The language form you are to use

You will be told to write a letter, for example, or a magazine article, a talk, a report, a diary entry or a debate speech. Clearly this is most important information since:

- It may affect what you choose to include in your summary: an eyewitness statement for the police, for instance, would need to be more precise about times, dates and locations than would normally be thought necessary in a diary entry or a letter to a friend.

- It will, of course, decide the *format* in which you present your material. Reports, for example, should be signed and dated and they require a title (possibly sub-headings as well) — though a title suitable for a report (eg *Children and television: an analysis of the viewing preferences of primary school pupils*) would hardly be appropriate for a newspaper or magazine article. If it is a letter you are asked to write, then you must provide at least one address, a date, a matching salutation and subscription (eg *Dear Sir, . . . Yours faithfully,*) and normally a short introductory paragraph serving to indicate the reason you are writing. You need to make yourself thoroughly familiar with conventions of this kind.

- It will enable you to judge how best to express the material you are summarising. The factual, objective nature of most reports calls for language which is subdued, impersonal and reasonably formal; a magazine article in the same style would make dull reading. If the summary is to be a talk or speech, your presentation will need to take account of the fact that most of us do not find it easy to grasp detailed or difficult information at one hearing, if only because we are more readily distracted from the spoken word than the written.

The 'audience' for whom you are writing

You will be provided with facts concerning the person or people you should imagine yourself addressing: their age, perhaps, or their relationship to you, or how much of the information in the passage they can be assumed to know already. Such details will help you decide:

- What material from the passage you ought to summarise. A talk on some aspect of your school, if it is to be delivered to members of your class, may take for granted certain information which would have to be explained if you were speaking to an audience of outsiders.

- The most suitable language level at which to write. An article intended for a children's magazine will naturally require simpler vocabulary and less complex sentences than one on the same subject meant for an educated, adult readership.

- The degree of formality and the manner or tone it will be most fitting for you to adopt. Of course, a job-application to a prospective employer will be more formally and respectfully worded than will a letter to a friend.

- The most appropriate general presentation of your information. The same facts will be treated very differently in two news items, one to be broadcast on Radio One and the other on Radio Four.

The purpose for which you are writing

There is always some point to our use of language on any particular occasion, something we want our words to achieve. It may be something relatively simple like getting little sister to shut the door or to see clearly why drinking the bleach would not be a good idea. But our aim may be more ambitious: to gain compensation for a ruined holiday, perhaps, or to win support for a scheme we have, or to give a version of an accident that subtly shifts the blame from ourselves. The instructions will specify or imply some such purpose and you must decide how it is best achieved.

Assume you are asked to write a letter (*language form*) to a friend who intends to leave school at 16 ('*audience*') with the aim of getting him to change his mind (*purpose*). Whether or not your letter has the desired effect will depend on:

- Your selection of information from the passage. Naturally, you will want to summarise whatever the passage has to say about the disadvantages of early school-leaving, whilst ignoring or being dismissive of any supposed advantages mentioned.

- The tone you adopt — one least likely to antagonise your friend. As a way of persuading someone to see sense, 'You must be crazy!' has less to be said for it than 'Don't you think it might be better if . . .?' You will probably want to convey a sympathetic and understanding attitude, and you might well judge that some show of embarrassed re-

luctance to oppose your friend's intentions would make
your advice more acceptable.

- The presentation of your case, bearing in mind that an
argument which is put badly will very likely convince no-
one. Your friend will probably not be impressed by a
collection of very general statements of the sort: 'Employment opportunities open to early school-leavers are
limited.' Instead, your material should be directed towards
the reader's own particular situation, each of your points
should be clearly contributing to the conclusion you want
him to accept, and you should try to develop a continuous
line of reasoning with the aid of connecting words like
those mentioned under *Coherence and continuity* on page
viii. Individual points should be made in as telling and
impressive a way as possible: you might consider, for example, how effective the use of contrast can be ('I suppose
you have to choose between a dead-end job next July and
starting a really worthwhile career later.'); or you might
want to formulate one of your points as a question which
practically answers itself ('Can you be sure any job you're
lucky enough to get in July will prove satisfying in the long
run?')

The attitude or feelings your writing should convey
The instructions may require your summary to reflect a certain attitude or state of mind: you may be asked to write a
letter of complaint, for example, which expresses *disappoint-
ment, anxiety* or *controlled anger*, or an article on modern fash-
ions which reveals your *disapproval, amusement* or *enthusiasm*,
or a diary entry which communicates *sadness, fear* or *self-
satisfaction*.

Of course, the way we express ourselves may tell our 'audience' a great deal about our feelings. Most straightforwardly,
this is because we simply state such information: 'I am *sur-
prised/relieved/happy/annoyed/puzzled/shocked* to hear that
. . .' But our frame of mind may be rather less directly,
though just as clearly, revealed, perhaps through our use of
a single adverb: '*Unfortunately/Thankfully/Obviously/Amazingly*,
she says that . . .', 'They have *foolishly/wisely/
selfishly/unaccountably* refused to . . .'; or through our choice
of some exclamatory expression like 'How *odd/ridiculous/
awful/funny/nice/sad* that . . .!'

However, you should give some thought to the more complex or subtle ways language can indicate feelings; how, for instance, the harmless request for information 'Do you intend to . . .?' immediately becomes a very different utterance when one of these adverbs is inserted: 'Do you *actually/seriously/honestly* intend to . . .?'; or when it is phrased thus: 'Can you really be intending to . . .?', 'Surely you do not intend to . . .?', 'Are you telling me you intend to . . .?' To take another example, what do we learn about the speaker's expectations and attitude from which of the standard constructions he chooses for a question: 'Are you leaving now?', 'You are leaving now, are you?', 'You are leaving now, aren't you?', 'You aren't leaving now, are you?'

As a final illustration, consider how, when describing a state of affairs, we often select one from a cluster of adjectives, all fitting the facts but each carrying a different strength of approval or disapproval: 'Your manner was very *easygoing/relaxed/casual/off-hand/negligent*.' 'She is *thrifty/careful about money/mean/tight-fisted/miserly*.' 'You will find him a very *honest/forthright/outspoken/tactless/rude* person.'

From all that has now been said, you will see how challenging these directed writing exercises can be, demanding as they do a good deal of sensitivity to the ways language operates in real situations. You should find the work not only interesting but most useful: the ability to be flexible in your writing and speaking, fitting what you say and the way you say it to the particular situation, this is certainly one of the most valuable skills the study of English has to offer you.

1 Followers of fashion

This is an eye-witness report written by a fifteen-year-old.

As I wandered around the town's shopping precinct a group
of people around the age of thirteen caught my eye; they
were jumping up and down, shouting abuse and generally
making a nuisance of themselves. I disregarded them from my
5   mind and thought no more about them.
Later on, I saw another group wearing tidy clothes, they
all spoke and were very polite. I carried on with my shopping
and after about an hour or so I noticed the two groups of
lads standing in the park just outside my house. I went
10 inside and watched the occurrence from the kitchen window.
Firstly I saw two of the lads from the untidy skin 'ead
group slowly advance on two of the mods, I noticed that
strapped to their braces were sheath knives which they got
out and started to threaten with. That was when the
15 fighting really took place. There was blood dropping on the
grass and bodies struggling with each other. I made my way
to my telephone and dialled treble nine for the police and
told them what they were doing to each other in as much
detail that I could remember. The young boys who were hurt
20 were taken to the Northampton General Hospital and those
left were taken to the police station to answer a few
questions. One of the lads I saw a few days later had a
deep 'scar' on his left cheek.
I 'Dread' to think how the Youth of today will be in a
25 few years from now. It may all have changed by then but
there will always be the different groups of fashion who
will fight each other.

Linda Martin

Summary

1   In no more than 35 words, summarise Linda's first meeting with the two groups described in lines 1–7.
2   Describe the events later that day, selecting whatever seems relevant in the passage after line 6 and using no more than 70 words.

Directed writing

1   Assuming that Linda had been asked to give a *factual* account of what she had seen — the sort of statement that might be useful evidence in a court of law — then there are certainly weaknesses in her report. Decide what you think these weaknesses are, and then improve the report, adding nothing to the information given in the original and using no more than 120 words.
2   Imagine that you are a girl or boy member of one of the gangs and have been asked soon after the fight to provide a written statement about the events described in the passage. Assume that you saw the other group in the precinct but had nothing to do with them until the meeting in the park. You have been told to keep to the facts but, of course, how you present the facts will depend on which group you belonged to.

   Do not add to the information given in the passage; obviously the material concerning Linda herself will not be included in your report. Use no more than 95 words.

2 Sold like hogs

In the early 1830s Elizabeth Keckley was born into slavery in the United States and remained a slave for thirty years until she was able to buy her freedom. This short extract is taken from her autobiography.

When I was about seven years old I witnessed, for the first time, the sale of a human being. We were living at Prince Edward, in Virginia, and master had just purchased his hogs for the winter, for which he was unable to pay in full. To
5   escape from his embarrassment it was necessary to sell one of the slaves. Little Joe, the son of the cook, was selected as the victim. His mother was ordered to dress him up in his Sunday clothes, and send him to the house. He came in with a bright face, was placed on the scales, and was sold, like the
10   hogs, at so much per pound. His mother was kept in ignorance of the transaction, but her suspicions were aroused. When her son started for Petersburgh in the wagon, the truth began to dawn upon her mind, and she pleaded piteously that her boy should not be taken from her; but master quieted her
15   by telling her that he was simply going to town with the wagon, and would be back in the morning. Morning came, but little Joe did not return to his mother. Morning after morning passed, and the mother went down to the grave without ever seeing her child again.
20   One day she was whipped for grieving for her lost boy. Colonel Burwell never liked to see one of his slaves wear a sorrowful face, and those who offended in this particular way were always punished. Alas! the sunny face of the slave is not always an indication of sunshine in the heart.

ELIZABETH KECKLEY
Behind the Scenes

Summary

1 Without mentioning anything of the mother's reactions, summarise in no more than 45 words the facts of this case as they are described in the first paragraph (lines 1–19).
2 What part did the mother play in the story and how did Colonel Burwell behave towards her? Do not use more than 55 words.

Directed writing

1 Retell the events described in the passage as they might appear in a journal written by the mother some years later. Of course, you will tell the story from her point of view, but add nothing to the information in the passage. Use no more than 90 words.
2 If Colonel Burwell had written an autobiography, what might have been his version of this episode? Do not add to the facts given in the passage or leave out anything important. Naturally, however, you will try to avoid giving the impression that you were unfeeling and brutal. Use no more than 100 words.

3 The trumpet volunteer

This is part of a radio interview given in the fifties by the rock musician, Johnny Iron.

INTERVIEWER   Well now, Mr Iron, what are your plans for the future?

IRON   Well, I reckon I'm going to stick around doing what I am for a while: rocking and rolling, and singing and all that sort of stuff. And then I'd like to leave that part of the show business altogether and I'd like to branch out in the straight side, you know. I'd like to have a go at the old straight acting there. I want to throw off this guitar. I mean, walking around with that around your neck all the time — people get sick and tired of that.

INTERVIEWER   Do you find it a hindrance, this guitar, for you?

IRON   Well, I wouldn't say it's a hindrance. I mean, I can't sort of bite the hand that fed me. No, I'm jolly grateful and all that for what it's done for me: it's brought me up from nothing to, well, you know, a star of stage, screen and radio and that . . . and records, of course. But I reckon it's played itself out now.

INTERVIEWER   So what do you intend to do?

IRON   Well, we've been — some friends and I — we've been mucking about with some of the classics that the public don't know about. You know, some things that have been hid away in the archives for hundreds of years. We came across one the other day: the *Trumpet Voluntary*.

INTERVIEWER	Do you mean the *Trumpet Voluntary* by Purcell?
IRON	Yes, that's right: Purcell. Well, take something like that, you see, and get in quick with

35

it into television. You want to get in quick with 'em, otherwise you breathe a word around the Charing Cross Road and ten fellers have done it before you've got out your front door.

40 INTERVIEWER   And what do you intend to do with the *Trumpet Voluntary*?

IRON   Well, first of all we're going to do a new arrangement of it completely, get a nice sort of beat going behind it and . . . Well, you

45   know, something for the kids to do a bit of jive to.

INTERVIEWER   Do you hope to sell a lot of records?

IRON   Well yes, I sold a lot of records as it is anyway. As I was saying, I come up now to

50   a big star from nothing. My mother, I bought her a house in Epping Forest, just by the swamp there; and my dad, I got him a new 1932 Ford — well, 'new': I mean, it's done up but it looks new now. All out of my earn-

55   ings. When a feller like me come up from nothing and suddenly rocketed to stardom, you got to sort of keep your feet on the ground or people will go round saying you're a bit of a big-headed . . .

60 INTERVIEWER   Yes, yes. How very true. Tell me, Mr Iron, do you have any plans for further records of this nature?

IRON   Well, matter of fact, my managers and me are working on Beethoven's *Choral Symphony*.

65   I reckon you can do quite a lot with that. And we're doing Verunjack's the *New World* thing by Verjumerojack, and several other bits. A bit by Ravvle and some others what, you know, what are just out of copyright.

70   You've got to wait for 'em to be dead a few years. But then we're going to whip in and have a go at 'em, as I say.

Summary

1 Taking your material from lines 1–22 and 48–59, summarise in not more than 40 words the benefits Johnny Iron considered he had gained from his career in rock music and his plans for the future.

2 Using no more than 45 words, describe the musical project Iron was working on at that time. Base your answer on information in lines 23–46 and 60–72.

Directed writing

1 A shortened 'polished' version of this interview appears in the next newsletter of the Johnny Iron Fan Club. It contains most of the information Iron gives in the radio interview but presents it in the form of more neatly expressed answers to the three questions below. Write these answers; in brackets after each question are the lines in the passage on which your answer will be based and the maximum number of words you should use.

  a *What do you consider you owe to rock music?* (lines 16–22 and 48–59; no more than 40 words)

  b *How do you see your career developing?* (lines 3–13; no more than 20 words)

  c *What are you working on at the moment?* (lines 24–46 and 63–72; no more than 50 words).

2 A short article in *The Pop Scene* begins:

ROCK IDOL BRANCHES OUT

During a frank radio interview in which he spoke of his debt to rock music and his plans for the future, Johnny Iron unveiled his latest ambitious venture.

Having whetted the reader's appetite, the article goes on to provide details taken from the interview. Complete the article in no more than 95 words; do not include any quotations from the passage.

4 Spontaneous human combustion

The best recorded case is that of Mrs Mary Reeser who departed this life on the night of 1 July 1959. The next morning, her landlady took her a telegram, but found the doorknob to Mrs Reeser's apartment in St Petersburgh, Florida, too hot
5 to touch, so she went for help. Two painters working nearby managed to open the door and were met by a blast of hot air. They could see no sign of the plump, sixty-seven-year-old lady. Her bed was empty, and though the room bore signs of a fire, there was only a little smoke and a feeble flame on
10 the beam of a partition that divided the single room from a kitchenette. Firemen easily put out the flame and tore away the burnt partition. Behind it, instead of Mrs Reeser and her armchair, they found a blackened circle on the floor, a few coiled springs, a charred liver, a fragment of backbone, a
15 skull shrunk to the size of a fist, and just on the edge of the scorched patch, a black satin slipper enclosing a left foot burnt off at the ankle.

The case was investigated in detail by firemen, police scientists, doctors and insurance men. Appliances and wiring
20 were checked but no cause for the fire could be found. Strangely, there was no sign of fire except in the vicinity of the chair, but there it had been unnaturally intense. A mirror on a wall had cracked with the heat, plastic switch-plates had melted, and in the bathroom more plastic items were dam-
25 aged. At the inquest it was said that crematoria normally use a temperature of 2,500 °F for up to four hours to burn a body, and even then they have to resort to grinders to disintegrate the remains to the state in which Mrs Reeser's body was found. Assuming that a heat of this intensity was some-
30 how produced, why, it was asked, was the wall not scorched behind the chair, and why was a pile of newspapers less than

a foot away not burnt? The FBI released a statement on
8 August, suggesting that Mrs Reeser had taken her usual
sleeping pills and fallen asleep in the chair while smoking,
35 but experts testified that even if her clothes caught alight they
could only have burnt the surface of her body, and that neither they nor the smouldering stuffing could have produced
anything like enough heat to ignite a human body.

JOHN MICHELL and ROBERT J M RICKARD
Phenomena: A Book of Wonders

Summary

1 Taking your material from lines 1–11, explain why the
   painters broke into Mrs Reeser's apartment and what they
   found there. Use no more than 50 words.
2 In not more than 65 words, describe the action taken by
   the firemen and the effects of the fire. Take your information from lines 11–25.
3 Summarise whatever information between line 25 and line
   38 suggests that it was not an ordinary accidental fire that
   had killed Mrs Reeser. Do not use more than 40 words.

Directed writing

1 The police ask for written statements from a number of
   those involved in the case of Mrs Reeser, telling them to
   keep to the facts and not to express any opinion about the
   cause of the fire. Write the reports for:
   a one of the painters referred to in line 5, explaining in
      no more than 50 words why they broke into the apart-
      ment and what they discovered inside. Take your
      material from lines 1–11.
   b a fireman describing the action taken and the effects of
      the fire. Take your information from lines 11–25 and use
      no more than 65 words.
   c a police scientist, explaining in no more than 40 words
      why it could not have been an ordinary accidental fire

that killed Mrs Reeser. Select your material from lines
25–38.

2   Soon after the fire the police issue a short statement to the
press. It consists of three paragraphs:
  a the date of the occurrence and how the fire was
    discovered;
  b the action taken by firemen and the effects of the fire;
  c facts that suggest that it was not an ordinary fire which
    killed Mrs Reeser, though the possibility of spon-
    taneous human combustion is not mentioned.

Write this statement in not more than 145 words, pro-
viding a suitable title but not counting the number of
words you use for this. Do not add anything to the material contained in the passage.

5 Snakes alive!

The African python Charles Sweeney knew to be inside a huge baobab tree would make a handsome addition to his zoo; he was determined to capture it with the help of his two assistants.

We all searched the gloomy interior, which was like a large room, for the bole was more than sixty feet in circumference, but the reptile was nowhere in evidence and must have climbed up into the honeycomb fibre that still filled the rest
5 of the trunk nine or ten feet above our heads. Looking up we could detect a faint glimmer of light that we discovered filtered through the fibrous matter from a hole in the bark twenty-five feet up.

    I thought that perhaps we could flush the snake out from
10 the top either by climbing through the upper hole or by using smoke. The difficulty was that the lowest branches, which were alive despite being hollow, were fifteen feet up; there was a massive limb just below the upper hole, but there seemed no way of reaching it. The Land-Rover, that I often
15 used as a ladder, was several miles away.

    After a vain attempt to scale the smooth trunk, we did an acrobatic act. I bent over with my hands on the trunk of the tree; Younis climbed on my back, followed by Badr, by far the lightest, who stood on Younis's shoulders; after teetering
20 for a moment or two, Badr managed to reach the lowest branch and swung himself up. He climbed cautiously higher, for baobab trees are notoriously treacherous to climb, even large branches being liable to snap almost as easily as a stick of celery.

25   Badr peered into the hole but could see nothing. We then passed him some dry grasses that he placed in the hole and set alight, putting green leaves on top to make a smoke. I went inside the hollow bole again, and after a few minutes

30 a wisp or two of smoke appeared but no python. To be effective the fire needed to be below so that the smoke would
be drawn upwards, but there was a danger of roasting the
snake alive if we did this. I called Badr down and concocted
a new plan.

35 Inside the bole, Younis climbed on my shoulders. Badr
handed him a stick, which Younis used to poke at the layers
of dry pith above him. A thick flotsam of fibrous particles fell
each time. After a minute or two an extra large piece of fibre
fell away, and all was confusion. The python had fallen with
it and landed on Younis. Badr fled; Younis toppled from my
40 shoulders, knocking me to the ground, where we lay mixed
up with the python.

The unfortunate snake, now really upset, struck out forcefully and fastened its jaws on my forearm, but Younis
grabbed it by the tail and it let go again, turning on him. He
45 hastily released the tail but while its attention was focused on
him, I caught it round the neck. The indignant reptile, bat-
tling for its life, struggled fiercely in my grip, winding its tail
round my leg and pulling so hard that it almost freed its head;
I had to grasp tightly with both hands to maintain my hold
50 and I was afraid that it would dislocate its bones. I yelled at
Younis to unwind the tail from round my leg. Fortunately
he had enough presence of mind to obey this instruction, and
once the tail was free the python was unable to exert any
leverage and the struggle was over.

CHARLES SWEENEY
The Scurrying Bush

Summary

1 In no more than 65 words, describe where the snake was
hidden and the unsuccessful attempt to smoke it out.
Take your information from the first four paragraphs
(lines 1–33).
2 Including in your answer a clear description of the final
struggle, give an account of the way the python was eventually captured. Take your material from lines 34–54 and
use no more than 80 words.

Directed writing

1 Charles Sweeney records the details of the capture of the African python in his journal, using the headings given below. Write this entry in the journal; in brackets after each heading is the part of the passage from which you should take your information and the maximum number of words you should use.

   a *The location of the python* (lines 1–5; no more than 20 words)

   b *The first unsuccessful attempt at capture* (lines 9–33; no more than 60 words)

   c *The final capture* (lines 34–54; no more than 80 words).

2 Write an extract from Younis's diary in which he gives his own account of the story, the unsuccessful attempt to smoke the snake out as well as the eventual capture, including a clear description of the final struggle. Use no more than 145 words.

6 Nuclear freeze

Scientists from both sides of the Iron Curtain have launched
a campaign to warn the world of one effect a nuclear war
would have on our environment which had been overlooked
until very recently. We all know something about the de-
5 structive power of nuclear blasts and the horrors of radio-
active fallout; what the scientists now want to publicise is the
'nuclear winter' that would follow a war, even a very 'limited'
one.

The research which has led to their warnings began with
10 a stroke of luck back in 1971. Late in that year, the US space-
probe, Mariner 9, chanced to be visiting Mars at the time of
a freak dust storm. The probe was able to observe the effects
of the dust on the Martian atmosphere and climate and send
this information back to Earth. After careful analysis of the
15 data, scientists understood much more clearly the results of
atmospheric dust and can now predict with great accuracy the
tiny drops in temperature which occur at different places on
the Earth's surface after the eruption of volcanoes. The research has continued with the aid of advanced computers,
20 and American and Russian scientists have arrived at surpris-
ingly similar conclusions about the nuclear winter.

They are agreed that even a small-scale war — one in
which less than 5 per cent of the world's hydrogen weapons
were used — would have a devastating effect on our environ-
25 ment. The explosion of the bombs would fling many thousand tons of debris, smoke and soot high into the air. This
material would be spread by currents in the upper atmosphere until it formed a continuous layer of particles blank-
eting the Earth. The sky would turn ashen grey and we
30 would inhabit a twilight world; but this darkness at noon
would be much worse than merely inconveniencing and
uncomfortable.

The particles would absorb almost all the sun's heat before
it reached the surface and we would be plunged into Siberian
35 winter. Except for narrow coastal strips, the land temperature
would dive to −25 °C and stay below freezing for months.
How survivors of the conflict could cope with the addition
of sub-zero temperatures to their other miseries is difficult to
imagine.
40 Moreover, only 5 per cent of the normal amount of sunlight could penetrate the dust layer. Photosynthesis would be
impossible and plants would die. With the food chain broken,
animals would starve. Even in summer months, crops would
wither in the fields, grass would stop growing and cows,
45 sheep, pigs would have to be slaughtered: all forms of agriculture would be crippled. The long-term effects of this blitz
on the delicate balance of nature would be enormous.
Of course, these consequences of a nuclear war would be
felt far beyond the boundaries of countries directly engaged
50 in the conflict. We can assume that few bombs would fall in
the southern hemisphere but movements of the dust in the
upper atmosphere would ensure that the South was almost
as severely hit as the North.

Summary

1 In no more than 55 words, summarise the second paragraph (lines 9–21) so that your answer provides the back-
   ground to the present warnings concerning the 'nuclear
   winter'.
2 Taking your information from the second half of the passage beginning on line 22, give a clear account of the
   causes and effects of the dust layer in the upper atmosphere which would result from a nuclear war. Use no
   more than 75 words.

Directed writing

1 Imagine that as part of their campaign to warn us about
   the threat of a 'nuclear winter', scientists buy space in

national newspapers to publicise their predictions. They ask you to prepare a statement of 90–100 words presenting the most important facts from the passage in a form that is easy to understand and likely to make a strong impression on the reader. Give the statement a suitably striking title, and, of course, do not try to include everything in the passage.

2 The school's Science Club has organised a meeting at which members will give short talks on some scientific topic of their own choosing. You are asked to contribute and decide to speak on the subject dealt with in the passage. Write your talk in no more than 110 words, bearing in mind that what you write must be understandable to a young audience at one hearing.

7 Another thing about Ted . . .

Just as we were going in their gate he said: 'If my mother wants to know how I got all this tar on, it was your stick that did it, not mine.' Just like him, blames it all onto me. Pinches my stick off me and then says it was my fault. He was my
5 best friend, was Ted, but I hated him sometimes. He was all right, but he was awkward in lots of ways. He lived right down in the two hundreds, just past that black doctor's. Well, it was always me that had to call for him, never him that called for me. And he could hit you, but you couldn't
10 hit him. And if he ever got into cop it, it was always your fault.

Another thing about Ted, he was always saying things about people, but you just say anything about him and he used to turn on you. He used to come up to you and go: 'Do
15 you want this button?' and if you used to say yes, well he used to pull the blinking thing off your coat and give it to you, but if you said no, well he used to pull it off and throw it away. Then he'd go: 'Well, you said you didn't want it!' You try doing anything like that with him, though. You
20 never knew how far you could go with Ted.

'Hey, vaulting over your wall!' I said.
— Another thing about Ted, he always wanted everything to himself. He got out the vaulting-pole and started vaulting over their wall with it. I kept shouting: 'Give us a go, man!'
25 but he wouldn't take any notice.

After a bit he says: 'Vaulting over our front gate!' so I have to traipse out to the front gate with him and watch him vault-ing over *that*.

After he'd had it for ages, Ted let me have the pole. 'Only
30 one go!' he said. I went out into the street with it and took a flying leap over the gate into their garden. One of my feet just caught the head of a Michaelmas daisy.

'Aw, you've done it now, man!' cried Ted. 'Caw, look what you've done with your big feet!'

35   '*I – it's* nothing!' I said, getting nervous. I had only broken the head of one flower.

'Oh, isn't it! Trust you! Wait till my mother finds out, that's all. Well it was you. I'm not going to say it was me.'

'Not asking you to!'

40   'Not *off* to, so you needn't think I am!'

He got down and started messing about with this flower. It wasn't *worth* twopence when it was *there*.

Then all of a sudden he gets up and starts acting daft again. 'Anyway, we've done it now,' he said. He aimed his boot at

45   the broken flower and kicked the head clean off it. He got his vaulting-pole and started swishing it at the other flowers, just missing the tops of them. Then he starts doing it at *me*, swinging the pole about two inches over my head.

I called out: '*Mind* out, man!' Ted pretended to be out of

50   the lunatic asylum and started pulling his funny face. 'You'll *go* like it!' I said. He started squinting his eyes and lolling his tongue out and taking swipes at me with his vaulting-pole.

'Hey, two monkeys having a fight!' he said suddenly. I had to pretend to be a monkey and we started rolling on the

55   ground pretending to wrestle.

That started it, supposed to be only playing, but you try just playing with *him*. He was all right for a minute then he starts biting. He kept getting his teeth into my arm and worrying it. Well, it didn't hurt, but after a bit I noticed bits of

60   spit on my sleeve. I went: 'You–ou — look what you've done!' and wiped it off on his jersey. Ted went: '*Mu–ucky* devil!' I said, 'See how *you* like it!' and bending down to the ground I bit his bare leg. I bit a lot deeper than I thought and he shouted: 'Ge–et o–o–off, man! I'm *telling* you!'

65   I let go and I could see the marks of my teeth on his leg. I pretended to be a mad monkey and went: 'Grrrrr–*an*! Grrr–*an*!'

'You're blooming barmy, man!' said Ted.

I suddenly realized that Ted had got his mad up. I felt very

70   silly and stood up, laughing like you do at the very end of a joke.

'You just wait if I get blinking blood poisoning,' said Ted.

'Yar–rn — get away, man!' I said.

'Yer, it's all right for you!'

75 He kept going on about it, just because he'd got hurt for
once. Anyway, he finished up saying: 'And you needn't think
my mother's taking you to that pantomime, so you know!'
I was supposed to be going to the Theatre Royal with Ted
and his mother a week that Saturday. She used to take us
every year.

30 'Don't want her to, I can go on my own!' I said. I was
feeling hurt, but on the top of it, angry.
She's not *going* to, don't you worry!' said Ted.

KEITH WATERHOUSE
There is a Happy Land

Summary

1 What does the narrator consider to be Ted's main faults,
according to lines 1–23? Use no more than 60 words.
2 Summarise the boys' activities in Ted's garden, showing
how they got steadily out of hand and led to their breaking their friendship. You will probably find it convenient
to give a name to the narrator, in which case call him
'Ian'. Do not use more than 145 words.

Directed writing

1 That evening, Ian, the narrator, writes a fairly detailed
account of the events in Ted's garden for his diary, beginning: 'I'm fed up with Ted Patterson after what happened this afternoon.' It is quite clear from the account
how Ian's annoyance steadily increased and that he is still
very upset.
    Write this diary entry, taking your material from line
21 to the end of the extract and using no more than 140
words, not counting those in the first sentence given
above. Do not include any of the direct speech or try to
imitate the northern dialect which you will have noticed
here and there in the passage.

2 Ted gives his mother a very one-sided version of what
   happened in the garden that afternoon. He does not tell
   any lies, but he reports only those incidents which show
   Ian, the narrator, in a bad light, leaving out, as far as he
   can, anything he himself might be blamed for. His
   mother, Mrs Patterson, decides she must write to Ian's
   guardian, Mrs Wright, complaining about Ian's behaviour. She passes on Ted's version of events and ends by
   regretting that, in the circumstances, she will not be able
   to take Ian to the pantomime this year.

   Write this note in no more than 150 words; do not
   bother with an address. Try to convey Mrs Patterson's
   annoyance and the concern she feels about the bad influence she believes Ian is having on Ted.

8 Agony aunt

The following appears on the problems page of a teenage magazine:

*Please look at the photo
I'm sending you. It's me
and as you might notice,
my nose is a bit on the long
5 side. It preys on my mind
and I know I'm being
stupid and letting my
imagination run away with
me but I often think people
10 are laughing at me behind
my back. Is plastic surgery
a possibility?*

Gavin (aged 14)
Liverpool

15 Let me put your mind at
rest straight away: you
certainly aren't being
stupid. If this photograph
is genuine — and frankly
20 I'm still not sure you
haven't been playing silly
tricks with plasticene —
then obviously people are
going to be sniggering
25 behind your back. I am
only amazed they
apparently have the self-
control not to laugh in
your face. So there we
30 are: rest assured there's
absolutely nothing wrong
with your imagination.

As to the nose itself,
however, it's no use
35 beating around the bush:
that nose of yours *is* large
— it's *very* large, quite
possibly the largest real-
life nose I've ever seen. It
40 is a remarkably large
organ. But take heart: a
hundred years ago there'd
be frenzied mobs
following you around the
45 streets and you'd be
pursuing a career in

fairground booths and
travelling freak-shows.
You certainly have much
50 to be thankful for.
     However, I realise that
what you want from me
is practical advice. I also
realise that it wouldn't be
55 helpful for me to tell you
to ignore the problem —
not when you must spend
all your waking life
struggling to peer round
60 the thing. But I do
suggest you try to get the
matter more into
proportion, so to speak.
There's no reason at all
65 why your nose should be
occupying so much of
your thought — not when
you have ears like those
in the picture, there isn't.
70 I do recommend you look
at those ears – I mean
really look at them — and
I'm confident that your
nose will then begin to
75 seem a very minor
deformity in comparison.
     But you know, we
really do have to learn to
live with what the good
80 Lord chose to give us,
and as I see it, that
means, in your case,
forcing yourself to join in
the fun. For example,
85 why not try strolling
casually into a room full
of strangers and
announcing: 'Hi, I'm

90 Gavin. With ears and a
nose like these I'm a dead
ringer for Concorde!'
Hilarious remarks of this
sort will not only make
95 *you* feel better, they'll
give a lot of pleasure to
others into the bargain.
And take my word for it:
friends will think more
100 highly of you when they
see you grappling
cheerfully with your
disfigurement.
     On the question of
plastic surgery I have
105 taken expert advice and
am informed that no
reputable surgeon would
dream of taking the knife
to an organ which is still
110 growing. I am assured —
astonishing though this
may sound — that your
fourteen-year-old nose
cannot yet have reached
115 its maximum dimensions.
So I suggest you shelve
the idea of plastic surgery
for the present.
     Finally, one more word
120 of comfort: If nature
takes her usual course,
you can expect your nose
to begin shrinking after
the age of fifty-five or
125 thereabouts — though, of
course, you must bear in
mind that since the rest
of you will be shrinking
at the same time, it won't
130 actually *seem* any smaller.

Summary

1 What is Gavin offered by way of reassurance and comfort in lines 15–50 and 119–130? Use no more than 80 words.
2 Summarise in no more than 60 words the 'practical advice' Gavin is given in lines 51–118.

Directed writing

1 When Gavin reads the reply to his letter in the magazine, he locks himself in his bedroom and refuses to communicate with the outside world except by notes which he slides out under the door. One of these is to his parents, explaining why he refuses to face the world. He tells them about the letter he wrote and summarises the reply in a way that makes it clear how terribly upset he is. Write this note in no more than 175 words.
2 This is the beginning of a letter Gavin's mother sends to the editor of the magazine:

> Dear Sir,
>   I must complain most strongly about the shockingly irresponsible piece of journalism which appeared in your last number.
>   My son, Gavin, is unduly sensitive about the length of his nose and wrote to your problems page to ask advice. His letter was published together with a reply, and after reading this he locked himself in his room and has so far refused to come out.

She continues by summarising the agony aunt's reply, indicating what she finds offensive. She is obviously very angry but the tone of her letter is controlled and reasonable.

Complete the letter in no more than 180 words.

9 Saint Spiridion's feet

Gerald Durrell and his family spent some years on the Greek island of Corfu. During a shopping trip, the ten-year-old Gerald, his mother and his older sister are caught up in a crowd making for the church.

Saint Spiridion was the patron of the island. His mummified body was enshrined in a silver coffin in the church, and once a year he was carried in procession round the town. He was very powerful, and could grant requests, cure illness
5 and do a number of other wonderful things for you if he happened to be in the right mood when asked. Today was a special day; apparently they would open the coffin and allow the faithful to kiss the slippered feet of the mummy, and make any request they cared to. The composition of the
10 crowd showed how well loved the saint was by the Corfiots: there were elderly peasant women in their best black clothes, and their husbands, hunched as olive-trees, with sweeping white moustaches; there were fishermen, bronzed and muscular, the dark stains of octopus ink on their shirts; there
15 were the sick too, the mentally defective, the consumptive, the crippled, old people who could hardly walk and babies wrapped and bound like cocoons. This great multi-coloured wedge of humanity moved slowly towards the dark door of the church, and we were swept along with it, wedged like
20 pebbles in a lava-flow. By now Margo had been pushed well ahead of me, while Mother was equally far behind. I was caught firmly between five fat peasant women, who pressed on me like cushions and exuded sweat and garlic, while Mother was hopelessly entangled between two enormous Al-
25 banian shepherds. Steadily, firmly, we were pushed up the steps and into the church.

Inside, it was as dark as a well, lit only by a bed of candles

that bloomed like yellow crocuses along one wall. A bearded,
tall-hatted priest clad in black robes flapped like a crow in
30 the gloom, making the crowd form into a single line that filed
down the church, past the great silver coffin and out through
another door into the street. The coffin was standing upright,
looking like a silver chrysalis, and at its lower end a portion
had been removed so that the saint's feet, clad in the richly
35 embroidered slippers, peeped out. As each person reached
the coffin he bent, kissed the feet and murmured a prayer,
while at the top of the sarcophagus the saint's black and with-
ered face peered out of a glass panel with an expression of
acute distaste. I looked back and saw Mother making frantic
40 efforts to get to my side, but the Albanian bodyguard would
not give an inch, and she struggled ineffectually. Presently
she caught my eye and started to grimace and point at the
coffin, shaking her head vigorously. She was scarlet in the
face, and her grimaces were getting wilder and wilder. At
45 last, in desperation, she threw caution to the winds and
hissed at me over the heads of the crowd:
    'Tell Margo . . . *not* to kiss . . . kiss the air . . . kiss the
air.'
    I turned to deliver Mother's message to Margo, but it was
50 too late; there she was, crouched over the slippered feet, kissing them with an enthusiasm that enchanted and greatly surprised the crowd. When it came to my turn I obeyed
Mother's instruction, kissing loudly and with considerable
show of reverence a point some six inches above the
55 mummy's left foot. Then I was pushed along and disgorged
through the church door and out into the street, where the
crowd was breaking up into little groups, laughing and chat-
tering. Margo was waiting on the steps, looking extremely
self-satisfied. The next moment Mother appeared, shot from
60 the door by the brawny shoulders of her shepherds. She stag-
gered wildly down the steps and joined us.
    'Those *shepherds*,' she exclaimed faintly. 'So ill-mannered
. . . the smell nearly killed me . . . a mixture of incense and
garlic . . . How do they manage to smell like that?'
65 'Oh well,' said Margo cheerfully. 'It'll have been worth it
if Saint Spiridion answers my request.'
    'A most *insanitary* procedure,' said Mother, 'more likely to
spread disease than cure it. I dread to think what we would
have caught if we'd *really* kissed his feet.'

70   'But I kissed his feet,' said Margo, surprised.
        'Margo! You didn't!'
        'Well, everyone else was doing it.'
        'And after I expressly told you *not* to.'
        'You never told me not to . . .'
75   I interrupted and explained that I had been too late with
      Mother's warning.
        'After all those people have been slobbering over those slip-
      pers you have to go and kiss them.'
        'Well, I thought he might cure my acne.'
80   'Acne!' said Mother scornfully. 'You'll be lucky if you don't
      catch something to go with the acne.'
        The next day Margo went down with a severe attack of
      influenza, and Saint Spiridion's prestige with Mother reached
      rock bottom.

GERALD DURRELL
My Family and Other Animals

Summary

1   Taking your material from the first two paragraphs (lines
    1–48), explain and describe this annual occasion, giving
    some impression of the variety of people taking part. Use
    no more than 75 words.
2   Avoiding where possible any repetition of information al-
    ready included in your answer to 1, give an account of the
    Durrells' involvement in the proceedings. Do not use
    more than 105 words.

Directed writing

1   Drawing your information from the first two paragraphs
    (lines 1–48) and in not more than 85 words, write a short
    entry for the Corfu guide-book describing this annual oc-
    casion. Aim to convey something of its colour and liveli-
    ness so that tourists will be encouraged to attend.
2   Write an entry from the diary of Mrs Durrell or Margo
    in which she describes the events of the day. Explain what

was happening in the town, conveying an idea of the variety of people taking part, and then give an account of your own involvement in which your feelings are made obvious. Do not add to the information in the passage, and use no more than 150 words if you choose to write Mrs Durrell's entry or 130 words for Margo's.

10 'I don't go to the cinema any more'

These are comments made by members of the public to explain why they do not go to the cinema often or at all.

1   The last time I went to the cinema it was so cold I had to sit with my overcoat buttoned up to the neck — and still I was shivering.

2   All the cinemas within ten miles of where I live show the same film at the same time. There's no choice: you either take it or leave it.

3   What's happened to the good old *family* film? It's no wonder people hardly ever go to the movies as a family now. I'd be embarrassed to sit through most of the films that do the rounds if mum and dad were with me. *Snow White and the Seven Perverts* isn't my idea of good clean family entertainment — at least I don't think it would be.

4   Hard, musty seats, often torn, with the springs sticking out — it's like the Chinese torture having to sit in the local flea-pit for two hours.

5   Why should I pay cinema prices to see a film that's available on video or that will turn up on television a year later?

6   When you've paid for the seat, bought an ice cream and taken a taxi home because the last bus has gone, you're lucky to have anything left from five pounds. I just can't afford that sort of money very often.

7   Going to the pictures used to be a nice evening out: a warm, cheerful atmosphere, comfortable seats, music, two feature-films, a cartoon and a newsreel. You really felt you'd had a good time.

8 I think film-makers are wrong if they believe everybody is dying to pay to see sex and violence. Films like that are all right now and then, I suppose, but mostly what people want is to escape from all the ugliness in the world: *Pink Panther*, *E.T.*, *Chariots of Fire*, the *Star Wars* films — I'm sure these are the sort people want to see.

9 Somehow it doesn't seem to be as easy to get to the cinema as it used to be. We had four cinemas until a few years ago; now there's only one, and that's on the other side of town. I have to get a taxi home or ask dad to pick me up: since they changed the timetable recently, the buses stop running to where I live at nine o'clock.

10 The last film I went to had half-a-dozen murders — really gruesome they were — some pretty horrible goings-on in bedrooms, young people sticking needles in their arms and a suicide. It's nice to go out and get away from it all, isn't it?

11 When you compare the average cinema these days to the comfort of your own living room . . . well, of course attendances are going to drop, aren't they? What is there to tempt me away from my sofa and the television?

12 Both the cinemas in my town were showing Xs last week, so legally I couldn't see either of them — not that I wanted to. It seems to me that the great British cinema-going public now consists of a lot of shady characters in dirty raincoats. I don't go any more.

Summary

1 Summarise in not more than 60 words the views expressed above concerning the quality and variety of the entertainment usually provided by cinemas today.
2 If the opinions above are typical of the way people feel, why would the public still be reluctant to go to the cinema even if the programmes offered were more inviting? Use no more than 60 words.

Directed writing

1   You have been asked by the owners of a chain of cinemas
to write a factual report to explain why attendances have
fallen off in recent years. Base your report only on the
views expressed above, and remember that you have not
been asked for your own opinions or to suggest remedies.
You should provide a title indicating clearly the subject
of the report, which should be signed and dated. Do not
use more than 140 words.

2   An article in the school magazine claims that we ought to
be ashamed of ourselves for not supporting our cinemas.
This view annoys you because you believe the public cannot fairly be blamed for the plight of the cinemas.

    Write your own short article for the same magazine.
Refer very briefly to the view you are opposing and then
present your case against it, basing your argument entirely
on the criticisms expressed in the passage. Use no more
than 140 words.

11 Adrian Mole, freedom fighter

Friday June 5th

Miss Sproxton spotted my red socks in assembly! The old bag reported me to pop-eyed Scruton. He had me in his office and gave me a lecture on the dangers of being a nonconformist. Then he sent me home to change into regulation black socks.

My father instantly turned into a raving loonie! He phoned the school and dragged Scruton out of a caretakers' strike-meeting. He kept shouting down the phone. Scruton said if I came to school in black socks everything would be forgotten but my father said I would wear whatever colour socks I liked. Scruton said he was anxious to maintain standards. My father said that the England World Cup team in 1966 did not wear black socks, nor did Sir Edmund Hillary in 1953. Scruton seemed to go quiet then. My father put the phone down. He said, 'Round one to me'.

This could well get into the papers: 'Black socks row at school'.

Saturday June 6th

Oh Joy! Oh Rapture! Pandora is organizing a sock protest! She came round to my house today! Yes! She actually stood on our front porch and told me that she admired the stand I was taking! I would have asked her in, but the house is in a squalid state so I didn't. She is going round the school with a petition on Monday morning. She said I was a freedom fighter for the rights of the individual. She wants me to go round to her house tomorrow morning. A committee is being set up, and I am the principal speaker! She wanted to see the red socks but I told her they were in the wash.

Sunday June 7th

Pandora and the committee were waiting for me in the big

lounge of her house. Pandora is Chairperson, Nigel is Secretary and Pandora's friend Clair Neilson is Treasurer. Craig Thomas and his brother Brett are just ordinary supporters. I am not allowed to hold high office because I am the victim.

Washed red socks, put them on radiator to dry ready for the morning.

Monday June 8th
Woke up, dressed, put red socks on before underpants or vest. Father stood at the door and wished me luck. Felt like a hero. Met Pandora and rest of committee at corner of our road; all of us were wearing red socks. Pandora's were lurex. She has certainly got guts! We sang 'We shall not be moved' all the way to school. I felt a bit scared when we went through the gates but Pandora rallied us with shouts of encouragement.

Pop-eyed Scruton must have been tipped off because he was waiting in the fourth-year cloakroom. He was standing very still with his arms folded, staring with poached egg eyes. He didn't speak, he just nodded upstairs. All the red socks trooped upstairs. My heart was beating dead loud. He went silently into his office and sat at his desk and started tapping his teeth with a school pen. We just stood there.

He smiled in a horrible way then rang the bell on his desk. His secretary came in, he said, 'Sit down and take a letter, Mrs Claricoates'. The letter was to our parents, it said:

> Dear Mr and Mrs . . . . ,
> It is my sad duty to inform you that your son/daughter has deliberately flaunted one of the rules of this school. I take an extremely serious view of this contravention. I am therefore suspending your son/daughter for a period of one week. Young people today often lack sufficient moral guidance in the home, therefore I feel that it is my duty to take a firm stand in my school. If you wish to discuss the matter further with me do not hesitate to ring my secretary for an appointment.
>
> Yours faithfully,
> R. G. Scruton
> Headmaster

Pandora started to say something about her O levels suffering but Scruton roared at her to shut up! Even Mrs Claricoates jumped. Scruton said that we could wait until the letters had been typed, duplicated and signed and then we had better 'hot foot it out of school'. We waited outside Scruton's office. Pandora was crying (because she was angry and frustrated, she said). I put my arm round her a bit. Mrs Claricoates gave us our letters. She smiled very kindly, it can't be very easy working for a despot.

My father raged about the letter. He is supposed to be a Conservative but he is not being very conservative at the moment.

I can't help wishing that I had worn black socks on Friday.

Tuesday June 9th
My father saw Scruton today and told him if he didn't allow me back to school in whatever colour socks I like he would protest to his MP. Mr Scruton asked my father who his MP was. My father didn't know.

Monday June 15th
The Red Sock Committee has voted to give way to Scruton for the time being. We wear red socks underneath our black socks. This makes our shoes tight but we don't mind because a principle is involved.

SUE TOWNSEND
The Secret Diary of Adrian Mole Aged 13¾

Summary

1 In no more than 70 words, describe the incident that occurred at school on 5th June and the way Mr Mole reacted when his son arrived home.
2 How did Pandora respond to the incident according to the diary entries for 6th and 7th June? Do not use more than 55 words.
3 Give an account in not more than 110 words of the protest action taken by Adrian and his friends, the consequences of this action and the final outcome. Take your material from the entries for 8th, 9th and 15th June.

Directed writing

1   The governors of the school ask the headmaster to prepare
a factual report of the whole episode. He does so, summarising all the events of which he had first-hand experience, including his conversations with Mr Mole and
what he understands to be the satisfactory outcome of the
affair. Although he keeps to the facts of the case, naturally
Mr Scruton will want to present them in a way that shows
him to be a reasonable and fair man concerned about de-
cent standards.

Write the report, using no more than 180 words. It will
be signed and dated, and will have been given a title that
clearly indicates the subject of the report, though none of
these should be counted in the word total.

2   Before she goes to bed on Monday 15th June, Pandora
writes an account of the whole episode for her own diary.
Of course, she will begin by recording what occurred at
school on Friday 5th June and then will describe later
events *in which she was directly involved*. Her feelings at
each stage are made obvious.

Write this entry from Pandora's diary in no more than
200 words.

12 Village entertainment

Laurie Lee describes one of the concerts which used to be held in the village schoolroom every winter.

'For the next item, ladies and gentlemen, we have an instrumental duet, by Miss Brown and — er — young Laurie Lee.'

Smirking with misery I walked to the stage. Eileen's face was as white as a minim. She sat at the piano, placed the
5 music crooked, I straightened it, it fell to the ground. I groped to retrieve it; we looked at one another with hatred; the audience was still as death. Eileen tried to give me an A, but struck B instead, and I tuned up like an ape threading needles. At last we were ready, I raised my fiddle; and Eileen
10 was off like a bolting horse. I caught her up in the middle of the piece — which I believe was a lullaby — and after playing the repeats, only twice as fast, we just stopped, frozen motionless, spent.

Some hearty stamping and whistling followed, and a shout
15 of 'Give us another!' Eileen and I didn't exchange a glance, but we loved each other now. We found the music of 'Danny Boy' and began to give it all our emotion, dawdling dreamily among the fruitier chords and scampering over the high bits; till the audience joined in, using their hymn-singing voices,
20 which showed us the utmost respect. When it was over I returned to my seat by the stove, my body feeling smooth and beautiful. Eileen's mother was weeping into her hat, and so was mine, I think . . .

Now I was free to become one of the audience, and the
25 Entertainment burgeoned before me. What had seemed to me earlier as the capering of demons now became a spectacle of human genius. Turn followed turn in variety and splendour. Mr Crosby, the organist, told jokes and stories as though his

very life depended on them, trembling, sweating, never paus-
30   ing for a laugh, and rolling his eyes at the wings for rescue.
We loved him, however, and wouldn't let him go, while he
grew more and more hysterical, racing through monologues,
gabbling songs about shrimps, skipping, mopping, and jumping up and down, as though humouring a tribe of savages.
35   Major Doveton came next, with his Indian banjo, which
was even harder to tune than my fiddle. He straddled a chair
and began wrestling with the keys, cursing us in English and
Urdu. Then all the strings broke, and he snarled off the stage
and started kicking the banjo round the cloakroom.
40   The Baroness von Hodenburg sealed our entertainment
with almost professional distinction. She was a guest star
from Sheepscombe and her appearance was striking, it
enshrined all the mystery of art. She wore a loose green gown
like a hospital patient's, and her hair was red and long. 'She
45   writes,' whispered Mother. 'Poems and booklets and that.'
'I am going to sink you,' announced the lady, 'a little ditty
I convected myself. Bose vords und music, I may say, is mine
— und zey refer to ziss pleasant valleys.'
With that she sat down, arched her beautiful back, raised
50   her bangled wrists over the keyboard, then ripped off some
startling runs and trills, and sang with a ringing laugh:

Elfin volk come over the hill!
Come und dance, just vere you vill!
Brink your pipes, und brink your flutes,
55   Brink your sveetly soundink notes!
Come avay-hay! Life is gay-hay!
Life — Is — Gay!

We thought this song soppy, but we never forgot it. From
then on, whenever we saw the Baroness in the lanes we used
60   to bawl the song at her through the hedges. But she would
only stop, and cock her head, and smile dreamily to herself
. . .
The night ended with slapstick; rough stuff about babies,
chaps dressed as women, broad Gloucester exchanges
65   between yokels and toffs, with the yokels coming off best.
We ached with joy, and kicked at the chairs; but we knew
the end was coming. The vicar got up, proposed a vote of
thanks, and said oranges would be distributed at the gate.

The National Anthem was romped through, we all began
70 coughing, then streamed outdoors through the snow.

LAURIE LEE
Cider with Rosie

Summary

1 Basing your answer on the paragraph beginning on line
   24, describe in no more than 35 words Mr Crosby's performance and the audience's reactions to it.
2 In not more than 145 words, write an account of the three
   musical items — those by Laurie and Eileen, Major Doveton and the Baroness. Include in your answer a description of the performers' behaviour and, where these are
   given, their feelings and the audience's reactions.

Directed writing

1 The following is the start of a letter Eileen writes the next
   day:

> *Dear Suzie,*
>   *The concert last night was a great
> success. It's such a pity you weren't here
> to see your old friends performing; you
> would have loved it.*

She goes on to write two long paragraphs. The first gives
quite a detailed account in no more than 75 words of the
performance by herself and Laurie, in which her feelings at
each stage and the way the audience received the turn are
made clear. In her next paragraph she briefly describes the
items by the other named performers, mentioning the reactions of the audience where these are given in the passage.
She uses no more than 80 words for this. Then she ends with
a short one-sentence paragraph which 'rounds off' the letter.

Write this letter, adding nothing to the information in the passage.

2   Imagine you attended the concert and have been asked to write a review of it for the local newspaper. Bear in mind that articles of this sort are normally very good-natured: they 'play down', without completely ignoring, short-comings, whilst stressing whatever there is to praise. Take your information only from the passage and do not use more than 160 words.

13 'Grange Hill' rules OK?

In the early 1980s the BBC began 'Grange Hill', a television drama series set in an English comprehensive school. Although extremely popular, especially, of course, with younger viewers, the series certainly has its critics. These are the sort of opinions that have been expressed:

1 What I like about *Grange Hill* is the way it deals with exactly the sort of problems children do have in school. Girls do get 'crushes' on men teachers as Claire did in one episode I remember, every school has bullies like Jimmy McClaren who make everybody's life miserable, and overweight kids like Roland do get picked on. *Grange Hill* has got it dead right!

2 Whilst I recognise that today's youngsters do indeed speak in the slovenly, ungrammatical, slang-ridden fashion depicted in *Grange Hill*, I believe strongly that programmes intended for a young, impressionable audience should seek to raise standards and not merely reproduce and therefore encourage, as this series does, appalling speech habits.

3 There is already enough mindless prejudice against comprehensive education in this country. We can do without the BBC's reinforcing such prejudice by presenting an absurd picture of non-education and labelling it 'comprehensive'.

4 Most of us identify with the pupils of Grange Hill because most of us do talk and behave the way they do. Fay, Annette, Zammo and the rest may not speak the Queen's English but then neither do real kids — not many of those I know anyway. Also, adults may not like

the idea that their children are rude to teachers, mess around in lessons and skive off homework, but that's the way we really are — and that's the way kids are in *Grange Hill* too.

5   Generally speaking, the juvenile 'pranks' in *traditional* school fiction did nothing to undermine the educational process: teachers continued to teach and pupils to learn despite Bunter, Flashman and company. In contrast, the great majority of Grange Hill's inmates seem to be waging total war against the school itself: pupils are in perpetual conflict with authority, classes are disrupted, teachers defied and ridiculed. By depicting sympathetically this fundamental hostility towards education the BBC is behaving in a most irresponsible way.

6   I am impressed by the remarkably high quality of the acting in *Grange Hill*, especially the children's performances. The naturalness with which they speak their lines and the utterly convincing way they enter into their parts really bring the characters alive.

7   Those viewers who allow themselves to become enraged by the speech of Grange Hill's pupils would almost certainly *not* object to the 'spiffing wheezes', 'leggo me ears' and other abuses of language found in public school fiction. In reality, what such critics are finding unacceptable is the *working class* nature of the language in the series. Needless to say, such middle-class narrowmindedness cannot be taken seriously.

8   Is Grange Hill meant to be a comprehensive or a poorly run Borstal? Heaven help us if our youngsters get the idea that protection rackets, intimidation of racial minorities, bullying, breaking into premises after dark and so on and so forth are perfectly normal ways of conducting themselves!

9   I think my friends and I like *Grange Hill* so much because the school is a comprehensive — the kind of school we happen to attend. It's not just that it's *called* a comprehensive: it really does *feel* like one, with crowds of kids moving along miles of corridors, a mix of pupils with different ability-levels and from different back-

grounds, etc. *Tom Brown's Schooldays*, *Vice Versa*, *Stalky and Co* and other series like these are difficult to get into because most of us haven't got any experience of public schools. Grange Hill, on the other hand, is the kind of school most English children are familiar with now.

10   Criticisms of *Grange Hill* often presuppose that children imitate what they see on the screen. Must we assume this? Where the depiction of violence is concerned, recent research has been unable to detect any increase in the aggressiveness of young viewers. Is there any reason to believe, therefore, that, for example, simply hearing the admittedly unimpressive language in this series is enough to cause our children to lower their own standards of spoken English? I have yet to be convinced of this.

Summary

1   In not more than 100 words, summarise those features of *Grange Hill* of which viewers approve. Take your material only from the opinions in the passage.

2   What are the reasons given by viewers in the passage to explain why they object to *Grange Hill*? Do not use more than 90 words.

3   Basing your answer on opinions 4, 7 and 10, explain why some people would not take seriously the criticism of the poor language used in the series. Use no more than 80 words.

Directed writing

1   Write a short report for the producers of the series to explain why *Grange Hill* is so popular. Take the reasons from those given in the passage and bear in mind that you have been asked to summarise the views of others, not necessarily your own. Your report will need a title which clearly indicates its subject and will be signed and dated. The total number of words must be no more than 110.

2 Write a brief review of the *Grange Hill* series for your school magazine. You strongly disapprove of the programmes and want to make out a forceful but reasoned case against them. Take your material from the views expressed in the passage and do not use more than 90 words.

3 Imagine that the objection to the language in *Grange Hill* given as opinion 2 in the passage appeared in a letter published by *Radio Times* and that you are writing a letter in reply. You disagree with the opinion and will draw your arguments from views 4, 7 and 10. Do not use more than 85 words, not counting those needed for addresses, a date, 'Dear . . .' and the subscription.

14 A bunk-house brawl

Georgie and Lennie were American farm labourers. Lennie, though exceptionally strong, was mentally retarded and very dependent on his friend, George. Immediately before this incident, they had been making plans to buy a ranch of their own:

The door opened. Slim came in, followed by Curley and Carlson and Whit. Slim's hands were black with tar and he was scowling. Curley hung close to his elbow.

Curley said, 'Well, I didn't mean nothing, Slim. I just ast
5 you.'

Slim said, 'Well, you been askin' me too often. I'm gettin' god-damn sick of it. If you can't look after your own god-damn wife, what you expect me to do about it? You lay offa me.'

10 'I'm jus' tryin' to tell you I didn't mean nothing,' said Curley. 'I jus' thought you might of saw her.'

'Why'n't you tell her to stay the hell home where she belongs?' said Carlson. 'You let her hang around bunk-houses and pretty soon you're gonna have some'pin on your hands
15 and you won't be able to do nothing about it.'

Curley whirled on Carlson. 'You keep outa this les' you wanta step outside.'

Carlson laughed. 'You god-damn punk,' he said. 'You tried to throw a scare into Slim, an' you couldn't make it
20 stick. Slim throwed a scare into you. You're yella as a frog belly. I don't care if you're the best welter in the country. You come for me, an' I'll kick you god-damn head off.'

Curley glared at him. His eyes slipped on past and lighted on Lennie; and Lennie was still smiling with delight at the
25 memory of the ranch.

Curley stepped over to Lennie like a terrier. 'What the hell you laughin' at?'

Lennie looked blankly at him. 'Huh?'

Then Curley's rage exploded. 'Come on. Get up on your
30 feet. No big son-of-a-bitch is gonna laugh at me. I'll show
ya who's yella.'

Lennie looked helplessly at George, and then he got up and
tried to retreat. Curley was balanced and poised. He slashed
at Lennie with his left, and then smashed down his nose with
35 a right. Lennie gave a cry of terror. Blood welled from his
nose. 'George,' he cried. 'Make 'um let me alone, George.'
He backed until he was against the wall, and Curley followed,
slugging him in the face. Lennie's hands remained at his
sides; he was too frightened to defend himself.

40 George was on his feet yelling, 'Get him, Lennie. Don't
let him do it.'

Lennie covered his face with his huge paws and bleated
with terror. He cried, 'Make 'um stop, George.' Then Curley
attacked his stomach and cut off his wind.

45 Slim jumped up. 'The dirty little rat,' he cried, 'I'll get
'um myself.'

George put out his hand and grabbed Slim. 'Wait a minute,' he shouted. He cupped his hands around his mouth
and yelled, 'Get 'um, Lennie!'

50 Lennie took his hands away from his face and looked about
for George, and Curley slashed at his eyes. The big face was
covered with blood. George yelled again, 'I said get him.'

Curley's fist was swinging when Lennie reached for it. The
next minute Curley was flopping like a fish on a line, and his
55 closed fist was lost in Lennie's big hand. George ran down
the room. 'Leggo of him, Lennie. Let go.'

But Lennie watched in terror the flopping little man whom
he held. Blood ran down Lennie's face, one of his eyes was
cut and closed. George slapped him on the face again and
60 again, and still Lennie held on to the closed fist. Curley was
white and shrunken by now, and his struggling had become
weak. He stood crying, his fist lost in Lennie's paw.

George shouted over and over, 'Leggo his hand, Lennie.
Leggo. Slim, come help me while the guy got any hand left.'

65 Suddenly Lennie let go his hold. He crouched cowering
against the wall. 'You tol' me to, George,' he said miserably.

Curley sat down on the floor, looking in wonder at his
crushed hand. Slim and Carlson bent over him. Slim straightened up and regarded Lennie with horror. 'We got to get him

70　to a doctor,' he said. 'Looks to me like ever' bone in his han' is bust.'

　　'I didn't wanta,' Lennie cried. 'I didn't wanta hurt him.'

JOHN STEINBECK
Of Mice and Men

Summary

1　Summarise the argument as it involved Curley, Slim and Carlson. It is clear from the passage what had given rise to the quarrel before the men entered the bunk-house and this should be mentioned in your answer. Do not go beyond line 22, avoid direct speech and use no more than 80 words.

2　Without using direct speech and in no more than 110 words, describe the chain of events which began with Curley's misinterpreting Lennie's smile (lines 23–72).

Directed writing

1　The police are summoned and, by questioning those present, get an accurate impression of what occurred. One of the policemen writes a detailed report of the incident and the events which led up to it. He avoids making any judgements about who was to blame; his intention is to record all the facts that might be useful in a court case later. Included in these facts will be the quarrel between Curley and the others when they entered the bunk-house.

　　Write this report in no more than 175 words. Do not add to the information in the passage and avoid direct speech. The report should be given a full title and should be signed and dated.

2　Imagine you were in the bunk-house when Curley and the others entered and you witnessed everything that followed. The police ask you for a written statement describing the fight and the events that led up to it. They say they are interested only in the facts and do not want you to express any opinion about who was to blame. However, assume that one of the following is true:

a You feel strongly that Lennie cannot be held responsible for what happened to Curley.

b You are a friend of Curley's and see him as the victim of circumstances and the brutality of others.

In no more than 160 words, write the statement from the point of view you have chosen, not including in it any direct speech. You must not omit any important fact or add to the information given in the passage; of course, you must not tell any lies. However, your own sympathies will naturally affect the way you report the episode.

15 Killer bees

Africanised honeybees, better known as 'killer' bees, are on the way to the United States. By 1988, they are expected to arrive in Texas, and shortly thereafter in southern Arizona and California. By the late 1990s, they could be resident in
5 all areas having 240 frost-free days a year. There is no way to stop them.

This impending scenario stems from an accident that took place in 1957. Twenty-six swarms of African honeybees were accidentally released from a breeding experiment in Brazil.
10 They had been imported by a Brazilian geneticist who wanted to mate them with European bees (now used for honey production and pollination in the United States and Mexico), with the goal of producing offspring that were better suited to the tropics.

15 Chaos ensued when a visiting beekeeper removed a piece of wire mesh from each hive containing the imported bees after he noticed that the screen was preventing them from bringing in all the pollen they had collected. Unfortunately, each screen had served to prevent the queen bee from escap-
20 ing. (Normally a hive doesn't move unless the queen moves.) Within a short time after the queens' escape, the bees swarmed, took off, and flew into the forest.

In 26 years these small swarms, totalling about 52,000 insects, have produced almost a trillion descendants. These
25 Africanised hybrids have expanded their original range by 124 to 300 miles per year. In South America, where the bees have already established their presence, thousands of domestic animals — horses, sheep, goats, donkeys and pigs — have been stung to death; humans have died as well, although
30 the number of victims is uncertain.

But African bees are not the invincible diabolic force depicted in a certain Hollywood film. Their sting is chemically

indistinguishable from that of the European honeybee. Indeed both bee races belong to the same species, *Apis mellifera*,
35 and physically they are almost identical.

It's their behaviour that sets African bees apart from the northern members of their species. They are considerably more aggressive. European bees have been bred over generations for gentleness; they pose little threat, except to those
40 allergic to their venom. African bees, in contrast, have an extremely low boiling point. And if aroused, they may attack en masse.

The African honeybee, like other honeybees, releases several pheromones, or chemicals, when it stings. Any bees get-
45 ting a whiff of these pheromones zero in on their source, but African bees are more sensitive to smaller amounts of the chemicals. In the time it takes one or two European bees to sting, hundreds of African bees can materialise and attack.

African bees also seem to have a good memory for odours.
50 If a pig, for example, happens to annoy the bees, they may direct a stinging attack at any innocent swine that wanders into the neighbourhood a few days later. Such behaviour may explain stories of 'unprovoked' attacks.

The bees may be able to hear, too. They are clearly an-
55 noyed by noisy vibrations and will go after people on motorcycles.

In much of Latin America, killer bees have gained dominance over their European counterparts. With their biological clocks geared to the coming of winter, European bees inter-
60 mittently slow their reproductive rate and store honey. But for African bees, there is no winter and thus no need to store honey. Also, as wild bees, they live under the constant pressure of predation. As a consequence, African honeybees put their energy into producing more bees rather than honey.
65 They are also better at defending their nests from enemies such as army ants, armadillos and robber bees.

The enormous population explosion now occurring in the Americas results both from their extremely high reproductive rate and from interbreeding between European queens and
70 African drones. Because African drones fly farther than European drones, virgin European queens, which also fly farther on mating flights than European drones, are more likely to hook up with an African bee than with one of their own race.

75   And the hybrids don't inherit their mother's better nature. African behavioural traits dominate.

The dramatic impact of the killer bees may make good horror movies, but it is the potential economic impact of the Africanised bees that most worries beekeepers, crop growers
80 and scientists. In Venezuela, for example, which now has one and a half million colonies of Africanised honeybees, honey production has dropped 15 per cent in some regions, and many commercial honey producers have been forced out of business.
85 Just how Africanised bees will compete as pollinators with European bees isn't known. Africanised bees seem to prefer visiting flowering trees. Two big groups of plants likely to be adversely affected if African bees displace resident bees are the tomato and potato families, which depend on 'buzz pol-
90 lination'. In such plants, the pollen grains don't sit in the open on top of the anthers, as in most flowers. Instead, a pollinator has to grab the anthers and shake, or buzz, them vigorously to make the pollen bounce out. African honeybees, however, aren't efficient buzzers, and the native bees
95 that may be driven to local extinction are the sole hope of many plant species.

MARY BATTEN
Biologists Battle the Killer Bees

Summary

1 Taking your information from lines 7–30 and 57–76, describe the chain of events which will have led to the invasion of the United States by 'killer' bees and their taking over from the resident European variety. Do not use more than 100 words.

2 Why, according to lines 31–56, are Africanised bees more dangerous than the European kind? Use no more than 80 words.

3 In not more than 50 words, describe and explain the probable economic results of an invasion of the United States by Africanised bees. Base your answer on lines 77–96 and the first half of the paragraph which begins on line 57.

Directed writing

1 Imagine that you are taking part in a radio natural history programme as one of a team of experts which answers questions sent in by listeners. Among the questions is this one:

> When African bees reach the United States, why will they replace the resident European variety? If it is true, as I have heard, that their sting is no more poisonous than the normal bee's sting, why are the Americans so worried anyway?

You have been given the question in advance of the broadcast so that you can prepare your answer. Write the answer in no more than 170 words, using only information from the passage. Bear in mind that contributors to this sort of programme will usually try to avoid sounding too formal; they do not want to give the impression that they are simply reading out something they have written beforehand!

2 This is the first paragraph of a newspaper feature article:

> KILLER BEES SET TO INVADE UNITED STATES
> Killer bees are on the USA's doorstep. By the end of the century they will have colonised most of the southern states. The invasion is inevitable: scientists are helpless to stop it. All Americans can do is wait to see if their worst fears are realised.

The rest of the article summarises the material given in the passage, treating the subject in the dramatic style commonly adopted by popular journalism.

Complete the article in no more than 200 words, not counting those used in the opening paragraph. Explain the reasons for the presence of African bees in South America and their rapid movement northwards, and then make clear why the bees are a danger to life and to the United States' economy, presenting your information as it might appear in a popular newspaper.

16 A creative urge

One of the inmates of Blackstone Gaol is called up before the governor, Sir Wilfred Lucas-Dockery, who prides himself on his enlightened views on penal matters.

'God bless my soul!' said Sir Wilfred; 'that's the man I put on special treatment. What is he here for?'

'I was on night duty last night between the hours of 8 p.m. and 4 a.m.,' testified the warder in a sing-song voice, 'when
5 my attention was attracted by sounds of agitation coming from the prisoner's cell. Upon going to the observation hole I observed the prisoner pacing up and down his cell in a state of high excitement. In one hand he held his Bible, and in the other a piece of wood which he had broken from his stool.
10 His eyes were staring; he was breathing heavily, and at times muttering verses of the Bible. I remonstrated with the prisoner when he addressed me in terms prejudicial to good discipline.'

'What are the words complained of?' asked the Chief
15 Warder.

'He called me a Moabite, an abomination of Moab, a washpot, an unclean thing, an uncircumcised Moabite, an idolater, and a whore of Babylon, sir.'

'I see. What do you advise, officer?'
20 'A clear case of insubordination, sir,' said the Chief Warder. 'Try him on No. 1 diet for a bit.'

But when he asked the Chief Warder's opinion, Sir Wilfred was not really seeking advice. He liked to emphasise in his own mind, and perhaps that of the prisoner, the difference
25 between the official view and his own.

'What would you say was the most significant part of the evidence?' he asked.

The Chief Warder considered. 'I think whore of Babylon, on the whole, sir.'

30   Sir Wilfred smiled as a conjuror may who has forced the right card.

'Now I,' he said, 'am of different opinion. It may surprise you, but I should say that the *significant* thing about this case was the fact that the prisoner held a piece of a stool.'

35   'Destruction of prison property,' said the Chief Warder. 'Yes, that's pretty bad.'

'Now what was your profession before conviction?' asked the Governor, turning to the prisoner.

'Carpenter, sir.'

40   '*I knew it*,' said the Governor triumphantly. 'We have another case of the frustrated creative urge. Now listen, my man. It is very wrong of you to insult the officer, who is clearly none of the things you mentioned. He symbolises the just disapproval of society and is, like all the prison staff, a

45   member of the Church of England. But I understand your difficulty. You have been used to creative craftsmanship, have you not, and find prison life deprives you of the means of self-expression, and your energies find vent in these foolish outbursts? I will see to it that a bench and a set of carpenter's

50   tools are provided for you. The first thing you shall do is to mend the piece of furniture you so wantonly destroyed. After that we will find other work for you in your old trade. You may go. Get to the cause of the trouble,' Sir Wilfred added when the prisoner was led away; 'your Standing Orders may

55   repress the symptoms; they do not probe to the underlying cause.'

Two days later when the prisoners assembled for the usual morning service, they found that the chaplain, Mr Prendergast, was not there to officiate.

60   At last the hymn was announced. The organ struck up, played with great feeling by a prisoner who until his conviction had been assistant organist at a Welsh cathedral. All over the chapel the men filled their chests for a burst of conversation.

65   'O God, our help in ages past,' sang Paul.
            'Where's Prendergast today?'
        'What, ain't you, 'eard? 'e's been done in.'
            'And our eternal home.'

'Old Prendy went to see a chap
70   What said he'd seen a ghost;
Well, he was dippy, and he'd got
A mallet and a saw.'

'Who let the madman have the things?'
'The Governor; who d'you think?
75   He asked to be a carpenter,
He sawed off Prendy's head.

'A pal of mine what lives next door,
'E 'eard it 'appening;
The warder must 'ave 'eard it too,
80   'E didn't interfere.'

'Time, like an ever-rolling stream,
Bears all its sons away.'
'Poor Prendy 'ollered fit to kill
For nearly 'alf an hour.

85   'Damned lucky it was Prendergast,
Might 'ave been you or me!
The warder says — and I agree —
It serves the Governor right.'

            '*Amen.*'

EVELYN WAUGH
Decline and Fall

Summary

1 Taking your information from lines 1–56, summarise the
report of the prisoner's behaviour given to the governor
and then outline the governor's diagnosis of the 'underlying cause' and the treatment he prescribes. Do not use
more than 100 words.

2 In no more than 40 words, describe what happened the
night Prendergast met his end according to lines 65–88.

Directed writing

1 Sir Wilfred keeps a careful record of his cases, convinced
   that future generations will find them enormously interesting. Summarise the passage as far as line 56 in the form
   of the report the governor might have written. Describe
   the events which led to the prisoner's appearance before
   the governor and then record Sir Wilfred's diagnosis and
   the treatment he prescribed. You will be writing as Sir
   Wilfred and should try to convey, without actually stating, the high opinion you have of your own wisdom and
   daring originality. Give your report a detailed title, and
   sign and date it, not counting these in the total number
   of words, which should be no more than 130.

2 On receiving news of the killing at Blackstone Gaol, the
   Home Secretary demands a report of the atrocity and the
   events which led up to it. Write this report in no more
   than 160 words.

   You have been asked for a straightforward factual
   account, not for any opinion about who was to blame for
   what happened. However, you feel strongly that the governor was largely responsible. You cannot include this
   opinion in your report, but you emphasise certain facts
   and refer to them in such a way that Sir Wilfred's guilt,
   though unstated, is obvious. Give the report a full title,
   and sign and date it, but do not count these in the word
   total.

17 A discussion: the earnings of pop stars

A   The enormous sums many of these pop stars 'earn' is quite ridiculous — in any sane society it just wouldn't be possible.

B   Why do you say that?

5 A   For one thing: it's incredibly unfair.

B   You mean they get more than they're worth?

A   Of course they do. Many times more than they're worth.

B   The problem about saying that is how you could ever go about deciding what someone's work is worth. As far as
10   I can see, the only guide to what's fair pay for a given piece of work is what people are prepared to give somebody for doing it. If the public is ready to give a sixteen-year-old twenty thousand pounds for a concert, then that's exactly how much that teenager's two-hour shift is
15   worth. People are happy to pay that amount so there's nothing unfair about it.

A   That really is nonsense. How can it be right to pay a singer more for a single performance than a trained nurse gets in two years? Obviously it isn't fair.

20 B   Well, explain why.

A   Any sensible person would see that when it comes to deciding how much pay a person ought to get for a certain job you have to ask two questions: 'How important is that job to the community, how socially useful is it?' and
25   'How much training does it need to do the job?' If you look at things that way, then a pop singer deserves less than a nurse, a teacher, a social worker and a lot of other professions besides.

B   All right, if you want to talk about social usefulness: en-
30   tertainers make a huge contribution to public happiness,

don't they? What sort of a world would it be without music? For many people music is life's greatest pleasure. We know that precisely because they're prepared to pay so much to get it. What contribution to society can be

35   greater than making thousands of people happy?

A   There's some truth in that but you really have to be reasonable. I just cannot see how anyone can possibly expect to get such fantastic rewards. Human needs can be satisfied very comfortably on a fraction of the income these

40   people receive. Personally I can't see that anyone *needs* more than, say, twenty thousand pounds a year — of course, *wants* are something different again.

B   So what do you think ought to be done about it? I suppose there ought to be a law against it, ought there?

45   A   I didn't say that.

B   No, but what other way is there? You'd have to have laws laying down maximum pay for different jobs and I don't think that's right. That's dictatorship, interference with personal freedom. And then you must bear in mind these

50   two facts: first, only a tiny minority of singers and other musicians get the sort of money you're talking about, and secondly, most of those who do get to the top aren't there for very long. The pop world is unpredictable: you can be a star one day and find yourself doing gigs in village

55   halls the next. Where would they be without the money they put on one side during the good times?

A   Oh come off it! Your average pop singer putting something away for a rainy day: very likely! And that's another point: we're paying these fortunes to people who are often

60   very disreputable types — drug-takers and the like — and who have hardly any real talent. You can imagine them trotting along to the Building Society after every concert, can't you! More important though: by rewarding them the way we do, we give them a stamp of approval they

65   ought not to have; we're encouraging our youngsters to look up to them and copy them. What we're saying in effect is: don't bother to make the best of your abilities, don't bother to take your schooling seriously. There's no need. Leave school at sixteen, buy a guitar and the world

70   is yours, my son.

B   For the sake of argument I'll agree that pop stars are no angels and are sometimes short on genuine talent. But

75

80

then so are the vast majority of people, aren't they? Most of us don't wear haloes and aren't endowed with exceptional talent. The way things are now we ordinary mortals can feel that there's hope for us too: we don't have to be saintly geniuses to win success and the big money that goes with it. Now that's a very comforting idea to an awful lot of people and it wouldn't be right to sneer at it or to try to take it away from them.

Summary

1 The first part of the discussion (lines 1–35) concerns the idea of fairness as it applies to earnings. In no more than 90 words, present clearly the stages through which the discussion progresses in this section.

2 Summarise the argument B offers to show that pop musicians *need* their high earnings (lines 52–56) and A's reply to it (lines 57–63). Use no more than 50 words.

3 Between line 57 and the end of the passage the discussion centres on the type of people who are pop musicians. In no more than 70 words, give an account of the arguments used by A and B in this section, avoiding the repetition of any material already used in answer to question 2.

Directed writing

Imagine that the arguments presented in the passage were in fact those used in a school debate by the proposer and the opposer of the motion: 'The financial rewards received by pop stars are excessive.'

1 Write an account of the debate for the school magazine, summarising the proposer's and the opposer's speeches in two paragraphs totalling no more than 180 words. Of course, you will be writing as a neutral observer presenting the arguments of others.

2 At the end of a debate it is usual for the main speakers to summarise briefly their main arguments so that they are fresh in the minds of the audience when they vote.

Write the summing-up speeches *either* A *or* B might have delivered, using no more than 110 words. A straightforward lively presentation of clear arguments is the approach most likely to win support for your side.

18 A spot of bother on the terraces

Mick was immediately engrossed in the game. He did not care about its quality, he only cared about United winning it. He encouraged and advised them, abused the opposition and referee, and was in constant debate with surrounding
5 supporters about controversial incidents on the field.

Karen was less involved. The close, raucous shouting made her head ache and she was disturbed by the continual jostling, and what she suspected to be unnecessary pressure on her back. And when United almost scored and the crowd
10 surged down the terrace, she was totally unprepared and would have fallen if there had been enough space to go down in. Mick hauled her back up the steps and the goalkeeper restarted the match with a goal kick.

This happened with every near miss, and although Mick
15 told her to hang on, and she tried to brace herself and stand firm, it made no difference, and they were toppled helplessly forward down several steps. Leaning backwards, they forced their way up again; but never as far up as the step they had been dislodged from, which convinced Karen that they must
20 eventually be crushed against the wall at the bottom.

She began to dread United coming over the halfway line and became a secret Chelsea supporter, willing them to keep the ball at the other end. The crowd across there kept falling forward too, and the waves of movement down the Kop were
25 like shadows racing down a hill. Watching these surges made Karen feel worse, especially when a body was lifted above the heads of the crowd and passed down to waiting ambulance men at the front.

'Mick?'
30 The United goalkeeper rolled the ball to a full-back on the edge of the penalty area.

'Mick!'

'What?'

'I feel sick.'

35   The full-back passed to a mid-field player who had moved
into a space on the wing.

'What did you say?'

'I said I feel sick. I don't feel well.'

The mid-field player began to dribble the ball up the touch
40   line.

'You'll be all right.'

'I think I'm going to be sick. It must be that hot dog I had
outside.'

'It'll go off.'

45   'I feel awful. All hot and dizzy.'

The United player tried to beat an opponent, but the ball
bounced out of play off the other man's legs. This gave Mick
the chance to have a quick look at Karen before the ball-boy
threw it back. Her pallor was obvious even through her
50   make-up, and there was sweat on her top lip.

'You're not going to faint, are you?'

'I don't know what I'm going to do. I just feel awful.'

The throw-in was taken and United continued their attack.

'That's all I need, you fainting and me walking round the
55   side of the pitch with the stretcher. I'd never live it down.
The lads'd crucify me.'

'Never mind the lads. What about me?'

'What do you want to do then?'

'I'll have to go out.'

60   Mick turned and looked at her even though the ball was
still in play.

'You what? We can't do that!'

'I'll have to, Mick. I feel terrible.'

She leaned against him and rested her head on his shoul-
65   der. Chelsea regained the ball near the halfway line and began
an attack of their own. Karen closed her eyes. She was getting heavier on his arm. Mick stood her upright and turned
round.

'Come on then. But I'm coming straight back in, I can tell
70   you.'

And he began to force his way back up the terracing hold-
ing her hand. Most of the people that they squeezed past
hardly saw or felt them this time, they were too intent on the
game. They reached the top of the terrace and began to walk

75 down the deserted steps at the other side. Karen held the
hand rail and Mick held her arm.

When they reached the bottom, Karen sat down on the
steps and covered her face with her hands. Mick stood by
impatiently, looking from Karen to the backs of the spec-
80 tators framed in the entrance at the top of the steps. Their
gestures reflected the fortunes of the game and after one
particularly loud shout, and what turned out to be a pre-
mature raising of the arms to celebrate a goal, Mick became
increasingly agitated.
85 'Do you feel any better now?'
Karen shook her head without raising it from her hands.
'What do you want to do then?'
'I want to go home.'
'Go home! They've only just kicked off! You're going on your
90 own if you do, I'm telling you now.'
'Stop shouting will you? You're making me feel worse.'
Mick relented slightly when she started to cry, and he was
just about to sit down and put his arm around her when there
was an outburst from inside the Ground that could only mean
95 one thing.
'They've scored! Come on then, make your mind up. What
are you going to do?'
Karen stood up. She was still crying. The damp tissue in
her hand had changed from pink to crimson.
100 'I'm going home.'
'Hurry up then. That's one goal I've missed. They'll get a
bagful against this lot.'
Mick stopped on the pavement just outside the turnstile.
'You know where the bus stop is, don't you?'
105 Karen shook her head. She did not look at him.
'It's at the end of the street, just across the road. You'll see
it. You want the 84.'
She walked away immediately. She seemed determined not
to say any more, but as she drew level with a poster on the
110 wall advertising the next home fixture she turned round.
'I've finished with you, Mick Walsh. You're horrible! I
never want to see you again!'

BARRY HINES
Looks and Smiles

Summary

1 Summarise whatever material in the first 43 lines of the passage helps to explain why Karen was feeling increasingly unwell. Do not use more than 100 words.
2 In no more than 110 words, describe those aspects of Mick's behaviour which suggest that he was not properly sympathetic towards Karen's illness.

Directed writing

1 That evening Karen writes to Mick confirming that she does not want to see him again. She explains clearly why she was feeling so unwell at the match and then gives her account of what followed. She is obviously still very angry and wants Mick to see how badly he behaved.

   Write this letter in no more than 200 words. Do not add to the facts presented in the passage or change them in any way, but obviously you will see things very much from Karen's point of view. Do not count in the total the words you use in the address, the date, 'Dear Mick' or the subscription.

2 A few days later Mick writes to a friend to tell him that he and Karen have split up. He gives the reasons Karen was feeling unwell — Karen's letter to him (see question 1) has made these clear — and then describes subsequent events in a way that presents him as the model of patience and reasonableness.

   Write this letter, keeping faithfully to the facts in the passage but slanting them to give an impression that is more favourable to Mick. Do not use more than 190 words, not counting those you use in the address, the date, 'Dear . . .' or the subscription.

19 The grey seal

Feelings run high on the question of seal culling. At the time of writing, June 1984, the Government still has to decide whether action should be taken to restrict the number of grey seals in our waters. The views of fishermen and conservationists are voiced in this chaired discussion.

CHAIRPERSON Mr Ferguson, what sort of reduction in the number of grey seals do commercial fishermen have in mind?

FERGUSON We're mainly concerned with seals around
5 Scottish shores; that's where they're doing the most damage to our industry. The least we want are annual culls to reduce the Scottish seal population to 35,000 and continued culls to keep it at that level. The Scottish Department
10 of Agriculture and Fisheries was forced to abandon a plan of this sort in 1978 because of public pressure.

CHAIRPERSON What is the present population?

FERGUSON In 1976 there were some 50,000 in Scottish
15 waters; at the present time there are probably more like 60,000.

CHAIRPERSON So numbers are growing rapidly?

FERGUSON Certainly. The grey seal is hardly an en- dangered species; that can't be why the public
20 react so strongly to our proposals.

CHAIRPERSON Why do you think so many people object to culling then?

FERGUSON Well, you'd have to ask them, but it obviously has a lot to do with sentimentality. I suppose
25 the grey seal does look a very endearing crea- ture, especially the seal pup. But I can assure

you that there's nothing about the seal's *behaviour* that endears them to the British fisherman.

CHAIRPERSON   Do conservationists agree that the grey seal is
30   in no danger of extinction, Mrs Rees?

MRS REES   It's true that the total number of seals around
all British coasts is in the region of 85,000, but
what you have to realise is that these are probably over two-thirds of the entire world popu-
35   lation. So you see, the number of grey seals
worldwide certainly isn't large. The culls Mr
Ferguson is recommending — culls, by the
way, which employ methods which many people find deeply shocking — would reduce the
40   seal population to a dangerous level.

CHAIRPERSON   Perhaps we could turn now to the effects you
claim the seal is having on the fishing industry,
Mr Ferguson?

FERGUSON   These are the facts: each seal eats approxi-
45   mately fifteen pounds of fish a day, a total annual consumption of 210,000 tons. Probably
two-thirds of this quantity are species of fish
we are interested in commercially. In the absence of seals it is quite possible that we would
50   catch nearly half these additional fish. This
would increase the British catch by nearly two
per cent, worth tens of millions of pounds. The
industry is going through a very lean time at
the moment; we *need* that extra income.

55   CHAIRPERSON   Mrs Rees?

MRS REES   We've got to understand what Mr Ferguson is
saying. His point seems to be that this two per
cent increase in the catch would result from the
total destruction of the seal population. That's
60   not what we're discussing, is it? We're talking
about a *reduction* in numbers. Even on Mr Fer-
guson's own calculations, this would mean less
than one per cent increase — surely not a significant amount. There are certainly more ef-
65   fective measures fishermen could take: for
example, they could try doing something about
their own overfishing of stocks which is so
damaging to their industry.

70	CHAIRPERSON	Even so, you do agree that control of the seal population would result in *some* improvement in the industry?
	MRS REES	Well, it's difficult to be sure. Mr Ferguson says two-thirds of the seal's diet is commercial fish.
75	CHAIRPERSON	I believe that's the official figure based on analysing the stomach contents of seals.
80	MRS REES	True, but the seals they examined were killed in commercial fishing areas; naturally their stomachs would contain a high proportion of commercial fish. But actually we know very little about the diet of grey seals generally. Perhaps they really prefer the predatory fish that feed off commercial species — in which case, of course, they'd be helping the fishing industry, not harming it.
85	FERGUSON	Unlikely.
90	MRS REES	Perhaps, but even granting that a reduction in the seal population would result in a small increase in catches, this wouldn't necessarily put more money in fishermen's pockets. The value of a given weight of fish declines markedly the more fish are landed — so much so that where some species are concerned fishermen might actually find themselves worse off.
	CHAIRPERSON	Mr Ferguson?
95	FERGUSON	Well, all that depends very much on the state of the market at the time of sale. May I raise a different point? We know that the grey seal harbours parasitic worms which attack cod. Infestations of codworm greatly reduce the value of catches.
100		
105	MRS REES	Yes, that's true. However, the evidence is that the level of infestation in cod is not related to the size of the seal population; that's to say, although seals may well contribute to the problem, it's not a case of the more seals there are, the worse the problem is. Maybe eliminating seals completely would do a lot to improve the disease situation, but it's unlikely that merely reducing numbers in the way we're discussing would do any good at all.
110		

Summary

1   In no more than 60 words, summarise the commercial fishermen's objections to the grey seal and the action they wish to see taken against it.
2   What are the opposing views taken by Mr Ferguson and Mrs Rees on the question of whether or not culling grey seals would endanger the species? Use no more than 50 words.
3   How is Mr Ferguson's argument in lines 44–54 answered by Mrs Rees? Take your material from lines 56–93 and do not use more than 95 words.

Directed writing

1   In an attempt to influence public opinion, the commercial fishermen buy space in a popular newspaper to present their case clearly and forcefully. They want to make the public aware of their objections to the grey seal and win support for the action they wish taken.

   Write the copy for this advertisement in 75–85 words, taking your information only from the passage and presenting it in a lively way that will catch the reader's attention and be likely to gain his sympathy.
2   Having read the advertisement described in question 1, the conservationists write to the same newspaper, answering the arguments of the fishermen. Write this letter in not more than 180 words, using material from the passage to present a reasoned, persuasive reply to the fishermen's objections. Assume that your readers have the original advertisement fresh in their minds so that only the briefest of reminders of your opponents' arguments are needed. Do not count the addresses, the date, 'Dear . . .' or the subscription in your word total.

20 The Elephant Man

Joseph Merrick, born in 1862, soon developed an appallingly deformed face and body, as a result of which he was known as the Elephant Man. Deserted by his widowed father and after several years of exploitation by showmen who exhibited him in this country and abroad, he was eventually given refuge in the London Hospital. He received much kindness and understanding there and was befriended by a number of eminent people, including the Prince and Princess of Wales. He died at the age of twenty-seven.

The passage is written by Sir Frederick Treves, one of Merrick's doctors, and describes events which occurred during the Elephant Man's time at the London Hospital.

A burning ambition of his was to go to the theatre. It was a project very difficult to satisfy. A popular pantomime was then in progress at the Drury Lane Theatre, but the problem was how so conspicuous a being as the Elephant Man could
5 get there, and how he was to see the pantomime without attracting the notice of the audience and causing a panic or, at least, an unpleasant diversion. The whole matter was most ingeniously carried through by that kindest of women and most able of actresses — Mrs Kendal. She made the necess-
0 ary arrangements with the lessee of the theatre. A box was obtained. Merrick was brought up in a carriage with drawn blinds and was allowed to make use of the royal entrance so as to reach the box by a private stair. I had begged three of the hospital sisters to don evening dress and sit in the front
5 row in order to 'dress' the box, on the one hand, and to form a screen for Merrick on the other. Merrick and I occupied the back of the box which was kept in shadow. All went well, and no-one saw a figure, more monstrous than any on the stage, mount the staircase or cross the corridor.
0 One has often witnessed the delight of a child at its first

pantomime, but Merrick's rapture was more intense as well
as much more solemn. Here was a being with the brain of
a man, the fancies of a youth and the imagination of a child.
His attitude was not so much of delight as of wonder and
25 amazement. The spectacle left him speechless, so that if he
were spoken to he took no heed. He often seemed to be pant-
ing for breath, thrilled by the vision that was almost beyond
his comprehension. He talked of this pantomime for weeks
and weeks. To him, as to a child with the faculty of make-
30 believe, everything was real: the palace was the home of
kings, the princess was of royal blood, the fairies were as
undoubted as the children in the street, while the dishes at
the banquet were of unquestionable gold. He did not like to
discuss it as a play but rather as a vision of some actual world:
35 'I wonder what the prince did after we left,' or 'Do you think
that poor man is still in the dungeon?' and so on and so on.
     The splendour and the display impressed him, but, I
think, the ladies of the ballet took a still greater hold upon
his fancy. He did not like the ogres and the giants, while the
40 funny men impressed him as irreverent. He had little sympathy with the clown, but I think (moved by some mischiev-
ous instinct in his subconscious mind), he was pleased when
the policeman was smacked in the face, knocked down and
generally rendered undignified.
45   Later on another longing stirred in the depths of Merrick's
mind. It was the desire to see the country, a desire to live in
some green secluded spot and there learn something about
flowers and the ways of animals and birds.
     This involved a difficulty greater than that presented by a
50 visit to the theatre. The project was, however, made possible
on this occasion also by the kindness and generosity of a lady
— Lady Knightley — who offered Merrick a holiday home
in a cottage on her estate. Merrick was conveyed to the railway station in the usual way, but as he could hardly venture
55 to appear on the platform, the railway authorities were good
enough to run a second-class carriage into a distant siding.
To this point Merrick was driven and was placed in the carriage unobserved. The carriage, with the curtains drawn, was
then attached to the mainline train.
60   He duly arrived at the cottage, but the housewife had not
been made clearly aware of the unfortunate man's appearance. Thus it happened that when Merrick presented him-

self, his hostess, throwing her apron over her head, fled,
gasping, to the fields. She affirmed that such a guest was
55 beyond her powers of endurance, for, when she saw him, she
was 'that took' as to be in danger of being permanently 'all
of a tremble'.

Merrick was then conveyed to a gamekeeper's cottage
which was hidden from view and was close to the margin of
70 a wood. The man and his wife were able to tolerate his presence. They treated him with the greatest kindness, and with
them he spent the one supreme holiday of his life. He could
roam where he pleased. He met no-one on his wanderings,
for the wood was preserved and denied to all but the game-
75 keeper and the forester.

There is no doubt that Merrick passed in this retreat the
happiest time he had as yet experienced. He was alone in a
land of wonders. The breath of the country passed over him
like a healing wind. Into the silence of the wood the fearsome
80 voice of the showman could not penetrate. No cruel eyes
could peep at him through the friendly undergrowth.

His letters to me were the letters of a delighted and en-
thusiastic child. He gave an account of his trivial adventures,
of the amazing things he had seen and the beautiful sounds
85 he had heard. He had met with strange birds, had startled
a hare from her form, had made friends with a fierce dog, and
had watched the trout darting in a stream. He sent me some
of the wild flowers he had picked. They were of the com-
monest and most familiar kind, but they were evidently re-
90 garded by him as rare and precious specimens.

MICHAEL HOWELL AND PETER FORD
The Illustrated True History of the Elephant Man

Summary

1 Taking your material from the first paragraph (lines
1–19), summarise in no more than 45 words the arrangements which enabled Merrick to visit the Drury Lane
Theatre.

2 In not more than 50 words, describe Merrick's reactions
to the entertainment he saw at the theatre, adding nothing

to the information found in the second and third paragraphs (lines 20–44).

3 In two paragraphs totalling no more than 120 words, describe Merrick's visit to the country, taking your material from the second half of the passage, beginning on line 45. The first, longer paragraph should summarise how he was taken to Lady Knightley's estate and his reception on arrival; the second paragraph should be an account of how he spent his time there and the pleasures he derived from his stay.

Directed writing

1 Write an account of Merrick's visit to the Drury Lane Theatre as it might appear in his autobiography, summarising the arrangements that had to be made and the entertainment he saw. Try to convey his attitudes towards the pantomime, not necessarily by stating what those attitudes were but by the way you describe what was seen. Do not add to the information given in the passage and use no more than 120 words.

2 Just before he leaves Lady Knightley's estate, Merrick writes to a friend describing his visit to the country. He outlines the arrangements made to get him there and gives an account of his reception on arrival and the pleasures of the holiday.

Write this letter in no more than 140 words, not counting those you use in the address, the date, 'Dear ...' and the subscription. Do not add to the information given in the passage and try to convey the writer's feelings towards his experiences through your descriptions of them.

21 Holiday of a lifetime?

Fourteen-year-old Helen sees this advertisement in a newspaper:

FRENCH WITHOUT TEARS — THE SCHOLATOURS WAY
Scholatours have been in the study-holidays business for eight years now — and we think we've got it about right. Judging by repeat bookings, our customers think so too. We offer youngsters a two-week holiday of a lifetime in one of
5 France's most beautiful regions and the chance to improve their French the easy way: by living with and being taught by the French themselves. There's something we offer parents as well: complete confidence that their children are in the safest possible hands.
10 Our experienced couriers escort small parties in modern air-conditioned coaches to Châteaulin in picturesque Brittany, stopping off for a guided tour of Paris on the way. The families the young people live with have all been closely vetted by our representatives; so our boys and girls are sure of
15 a warm welcome, comfortable rooms of their own and lots of wholesome French cuisine — a home from home in fact. Of course, our couriers are on hand day and night to see that nothing spoils a perfect stay.
An exciting programme of trips to places of interest in the
20 area is arranged for the afternoons. And with supervised discos, film-shows and talks, there's plenty happening in the evenings as well. And the study? Classes are conducted every weekday morning in modern surroundings by highly qualified French instructors. The emphasis is on individual tuition
25 and language-laboratory work.
A holiday a youngster will never forget? Certainly, but much more. For parents: peace of mind. For their son or daughter: French without tears.
For more details, please write to: Scholatours Ltd, PO Box
30 58, London GY67 5BH.

Helen shows the advertisement to her parents. They send for more information, which is reassuring, though it adds little to what is said in the advertisement; and they book a fortnight's holiday costing £250 for their daughter.

At the end of the first week of her holiday, Helen sends this letter home:

>   12, rue Lafayette,
>   Châteaulin 12.
>
>   10th August, 1984.
>
> Dear Mum, Dad and Tim,
>   Things haven't gone too well so far.
> In fact, to tell the truth, the first week's been a bit of a
> shambles.

35
>   The journey down was a nightmare. The coach must have
> been borrowed from a transport museum. It broke down twice
> and was so small we had to sit three to a seat. As promised, we
> stopped at Paris – that's to say, we were dumped near the centre
> and the courier went off, telling us to amuse ourselves for a

40
> couple of hours. Great! We'd no idea how to get anywhere so
> we just sat in a park, ate the packed lunches we'd been given
> and waited.
>   We finally got to Châteaulin at 10.30 p.m. but there weren't
> enough families to go round, so I dozed in the coach till 9.30

45
> the next morning. Then I was taken to M. and Mme. Gigante's.
> They're very nice and have done their best to make me feel at
> home, but obviously they weren't expecting me. I share a room
> (and bunk-beds!) with their ten-year-old daughter, Dominique.
> I'm given breakfast and dinner but have to find lunch for

50
> myself, so money is running pretty short. I do try to last
> through to dinner but breakfast is only rolls and coffee so my
> stomach's twisting itself into knots by midday.
>   Don't reckon much to the tuition. Classes are held in a
> kind of grotty church-hall, a group of us in each corner. The

55
> teachers don't seem to know what they're doing. I think most
> of them are on holiday from college and they're not much older
> than us. No textbooks. We spend most of the time chatting to the
> teacher about this and that <u>in English</u>! By the way, the
> ultra-mod language lab. is a portable cassette-recorder!

60   Most afternoons we just wander round Châteaulin, which is very pretty actually, or sit in cafés. There's been one trip so far. That was to Quimper - really smashing that was. Hope you got my postcard. I think they're taking us somewhere else next week, but the courier says no other trips are

65   arranged.

The only thing they've laid on during the evenings was a sort of disco last Tuesday. BUT THERE WASN'T A SINGLE DURAN DURAN RECORD !! Mostly I've stayed in watching Dallas and Benny Hill (dubbed) on the telly.

70   We hardly see the courier. Well, we <u>see</u> her around the town but somehow she seems more interested in her French boyfriend than in poor old us !

Missing you all a lot. Give Tibbles a hug for me.

Lots of love,
Helen

75

Summary

1 In no more than 40 words, show that Helen's journey down to Brittany was not what the Scholatours' advertisement had promised it would be.
2 Summarise the ways in which Helen had been misled about what she could expect during her stay in Châteaulin. Do not use more than 120 words.

Directed writing

1 A friend of Helen's parents has told them that she is trying to book a similar study-holiday for her son. As soon as Helen's mother receives Helen's letter she writes to her friend to warn her against dealing with Scholatours. She outlines her daughter's experiences to show that the firm's promises have not been kept.

Write this letter in no more than 190 words, not counting those you use for the address, the date, 'Dear . . .' and the subscription.

2   When they receive Helen's letter, her parents are very angry and concerned for their daughter's wellbeing. They find they cannot get in touch with Scholatours by telephone, so they write to them immediately. They summarise the ways in which they consider they have been misled by the information they received from the firm and insist something be done promptly to put their minds at rest about Helen. They adopt a very firm tone and their annoyance and concern are obvious, but they are not abusive.

Write this letter in no more than 210 words, not counting those you use for the addresses, the date, 'Dear Sir' and the subscription.

22 Electricity from the sun

Dr Magnus Pyke considers the case for harnessing solar energy as an alternative to oil in the generation of electricity.

Given that much of the sun's power that reaches the outer atmosphere never filters through to us, it can be concluded that a solar-energy collector orbiting outside the earth's atmosphere would be far more efficient than collectors on its
5   surface. In addition, a satellite placed in a suitable orbit would be in a position to receive sunlight nearly twenty-four hours a day.

Each satellite would be fitted with large 'wings' covered with panels of solar-energy-receiving cells that would convert
10 the sun's radiation into electricity, in the same way that existing photovoltaic cells did on Skylab. The electricity would then be converted into a microwave beam directed towards a receiving station on earth.

The receiving station would be constructed from antennae
15 covering an area of 15.5 square kilometres. This would be large enough to collect all the power needed to satisfy the energy demand of a city the size of New York.

Critics of the idea argue that the construction of just one satellite would require the full commitment of NASA's space
20 shuttle system to carry all the pieces of equipment into orbit. Numerous other flights would then be needed to assemble the power station and ferry the crews who would be needed to work it to and fro every few weeks. These costs alone would be enormous, not to mention those of constructing the
25 receiving station on earth. Moreover, the microwave beam would be a hazard to any living creature on which it fell. Apart from flocks of birds that might inadvertently fly through it, a deflection of just one degree could cast the beam

onto the earth's surface more than 200 kilometres from its
30   target. An easier solution must lie nearer home.

The chief problem with harnessing the sunshine that falls
on earth is that it is very spread out. This means that any
system of collecting it would have to be spread over a very
wide area as well. One scheme aims to use fields of silicon
35   solar cells, which are cheaper to manufacture than those used
in the current space programme. These silicon cells would
produce direct electric current, which would need to be converted into alternating current before it could be fed into the
existing electricity supply system. The area needed by these
40   fields of cells is very large. One estimate claims that by the
year 2040, the projected demands for electricity throughout
the world would require fields of silicon cells collecting sunlight over an area larger than the whole of Yugoslavia.

The possibility of using a solar reflector has also been sug-
45   gested. Recently French scientists have constructed a solar
furnace in the Pyrenees capable of generating a temperature
of 4,000°C, which is hot enough to melt diamonds. Sixty-three
giant mirrors with a total area of 2050 square metres of glass
were spread over a hillside, reflecting the sun's rays onto a
50   furnace 30 centimetres in diameter. As the sun moved across
the sky, the mirrors turned with it to maintain a constant
reflection onto the furnace.

If such a system were to be used to provide power to generate electricity on an industrial scale, the reflector system
55   would need to be over 1,250 times as large as the existing one
in France and even then it would only generate power during
daylight hours and on fine days.

This introduces one of the additional problems of solar
power, the need to be able to store it for those periods when
60   the sun does not shine. Existing batteries and accumulators
are obviously inadequate. Major improvements will have to
be made before it is possible to store enough electricity to
power one domestic house, let alone an entire city.

Perhaps the greatest setback to the use of solar energy for
65   the generation of electricity on a large scale is that the sun
shines longest and most brightly on those parts of the world
which are least developed and often least inhabited. In parts
of the Sahara there are fewer than 100 hours of cloud the
whole year. Yet there is nobody there to use all the sunshine

70 and so far those people with the finance and the knowledge
have hesitated to invest in an expensive scheme so far from
home.

MAGNUS PYKE
Our Future: Dr Magnus Pyke Predicts

Summary

1 Describe in not more than 50 words the proposed use of
satellites to generate electricity, taking your material from
the first three paragraphs (lines 1–17). Include what is
said in the first paragraph about the particular advantages
of this system.

2 According to the fourth paragraph (lines 18–30), what is
there to be said against the satellite proposal? Do not ex-
ceed 45 words.

3 In two paragraphs, summarise the material from line 31
to the end of the passage concerning surface-based sys-
tems. In the first paragraph, describe the two schemes;
in the second, outline the objections raised to these specific proposals as well as those that would apply to any
scheme of this sort. Your complete answer should be no
more than 110 words.

Directed writing

1 A non-technical magazine aimed at the general reader has
asked you to submit an article entitled 'Alternative
Sources of Energy'. Using not more than 115 words, write
that section of the article concerned with solar energy,
describing the three schemes considered in the passage.
You are clearly optimistic about the prospects and mention none of the drawbacks.

2 You have read the article referred to in the preceding exercise and are not at all impressed by the proposals described there. Write a letter for publication in the same
magazine, using no more than 150 words, not counting

those in the addresses, the date, 'Dear . . .' and the subscription.

Drawing only on material given in the passage, raise objections to each scheme in turn and then mention those that would apply to any surface-based project. You may assume that your readers are familiar with the original article so that only very brief reminders of the schemes are needed.

23 Girls and science

A fourth-year discussion group has been given the following table and asked if anything of any interest is revealed by the figures.

Females as a percentage of GCE passes in various subjects (England and Wales)						
	O level			*A level*		
	1979	1980	1981	1979	1980	1981
Physics	25.0	25.7	26.3	18.9	19.3	20.1
Chemistry	35.9	34.3	37.7	30.6	32.7	33.3
History	50.9	53.5	53.4	50.4	51.5	52.3
Eng. Lang.	57.6	57.5	57.3	—	—	—
Biology	59.5	59.9	60.7	53.0	55.6	56.4
French	60.0	59.9	60.7	65.5	71.6	71.9
Eng. Lit.	61.9	62.9	61.1	69.7	69.5	70.1
All subjects	50.8	50.8	51.4	43.8	45.0	45.9

VICKY   The figures show what we knew already: girls tend to steer clear of the physical sciences — physics and chemistry — and go for languages, literature — subjects like that. Those are the subjects they
5   prefer.

GWEN   It looks as though the situation is slowly changing, though, doesn't it? The proportion of girls taking physics and chemistry is creeping up.

EMMA   Yes, there's a slight increase every year.

10 VICKY I don't think you're right — not when you look at that bottom line of figures. More girls are taking GCEs generally, so of course you're bound to get

		more doing physics and chemistry. It's not that girls' preferences are really changing very much.

more doing physics and chemistry. It's not
that girls' preferences are really changing very
15   much.

JOHN   No, and they won't: boys have got more of a natural aptitude for science — the physical sciences anyway. Girls just aren't cut out for them.

GRAHAM   I don't know that it's a matter of aptitude.

20 JOHN   What else could it be?

GWEN   It's because the physical sciences aren't traditional girls' subjects, are they? After all, a lot of girls' schools didn't even have physics and chemistry departments until quite recently.

25 JOHN   Maybe, but things are different now. Take our school: the facilities are there for girls to do science but still not many of them opt for it in the fourth year, do they? Why is that?

EMMA   Gwen's already said it: physics and chemistry are
30   still generally considered to be boys' subjects, the same way cookery is seen as a girls' subject. The physical sciences have a masculine image and so naturally girls are put off them.

JOHN   That's a very old-fashioned attitude.

35 VICKY   It may be old-fashioned but we're still encouraged to think that way. For example, children's books and magazines keep the attitude going. The message you get from them is even worse than the real world: whenever the story calls for a scientist, enter
40   a man! Always.

GWEN   And textbooks. Do you remember that sentence we came across? 'Marie Curie did what few people — men or women — could do.' Fantastic! She wasn't only better than most women, she was, mir-
45   acle of miracles, a better scientist than most men as well!

GRAHAM   It's a sort of brain-washing, isn't it? The scientists are naturally men; the secretaries, nurses and primary school teachers are naturally women.

50 EMMA   You even get that in careers lessons. Have you noticed the posters in Miss Roberts' room? The research chemists and engineers and physicists are all men; the nurses and child care officers are women.

GWEN   And those visits we went on last term were ar-

55 ranged so that it was the boys who looked round the ICI laboratories, while the girls trooped off to the secretarial college.

VICKY When Jenny Williams saw Miss Roberts about doing physics at university, most of the time was
60 spent with Jenny being told all the difficulties she'd meet getting a job afterwards. It was discouraging.

JOHN But that's just being realistic, isn't it? It does tend to be more difficult for girls to get jobs in physics and chemistry. It may be unfair but it's true.

65 VICKY Can't you see, though, that if the problems are stressed, girls will continue to be put off and nothing is going to change? It's a sort of vicious circle.

GRAHAM I reckon what you need is some brain-washing in reverse. There are more women scientists than just
70 Madame Curie: why aren't there posters of them up in the labs?

EMMA And we could have visits from women who've made their careers in science; they could come and talk to us about their work — preferably attractive,
75 married women to show that you don't have to stop being feminine to be a scientist. Things like this would help to get rid of the masculine image science has got.

GWEN Another thing: when I arrived at this school I was
80 quite keen on science, and I've remained interested in biology . . .

JOHN Yes, the figures show girls go for that science. I wonder why that is.

GWEN Anyway, one reason I began straight away to see
85 physics and chemistry as boys' subjects was that the boys seemed to be much more at home with them from the word 'go'. For example, the boys seemed to know quite a bit about electricity already; I didn't.

90 JOHN That's to do with the way boys spend their time outside school. Quite early on boys will be tinkering with motors, mending fuses and so on. Most parents encourage it.

EMMA While their sisters are expected to be organising
95 dolls' tea-parties and shampooing the hamster! My parents would still have a fit if they saw me wiring a plug.

100	GRAHAM	It's true. And boys are given chemistry sets for Christmas and construction kits. They do start off with an advantage, I can see that. I suppose teachers ought to take this into account and give girls special encouragement.
105	VICKY	Certainly parents do influence the way we think about science. When I discussed my options with mum and dad last year, they just seemed to assume I'd drop physics and chemistry, even though my marks had been quite good.
	GWEN	Even teachers.
110	JOHN	They aren't allowed to stop girls doing science — not now there's the Sex Discrimination Act.
115	GWEN	No, it doesn't work like that; it's a matter of attitude again. In a mixed school like this one, where only a certain number of us can opt for O-level science, teachers, like parents, just assume it will be the boys who will want to take up the places. I don't suppose they realise what they're doing, but they do give you the impression that science is more for the boys.
120	EMMA	You see it in lots of little ways. Did you notice, for example, that when there was a shortage of apparatus in physics practicals, somehow it was always the boys who got the chance to use it?
125	VICKY	And when there weren't enough places at the proper benches in chemistry, it was usually the girls who had to sit at the side benches facing the wall.
	JOHN	That's because girls don't push themselves forward.
130	GRAHAM	Right, they don't have the confidence in these subjects. That's why they need special encouragement.

Summary

1   In no more than 60 words, summarise information contained in the table which shows how markedly different are the choices boys and girls make concerning which GCE subjects to study, and whether or not these attitudes are changing.

2 According to the discussion, why can parents be held partly responsible for the fact that fewer girls than boys opt for the physical sciences? Use no more than 60 words.

3 In two paragraphs totalling no more than 95 words, summarise what is said in the passage concerning the ways in which:

   a some teachers reinforce the 'male image' of the physical sciences.

   b that image could be changed.

Directed writing

1 Having heard the discussion, you decide to write an article for the school magazine on the subject of girls and the physical sciences. You want simply to explain why relatively few girls opt for physics and chemistry, not to make any recommendations.

   Begin by summarising any information in the table which seems to you to present the situation clearly and then offer your explanations. Restrict yourself to the material in the passage and use no more than 190 words.

2 Write a leaflet entitled *Girls and the Physical Sciences: the role of the teacher*, which will be displayed on staffroom noticeboards. Your intention is to win the support of teachers in encouraging girls to opt for physics and chemistry. The leaflet, which must be no longer than 190 words, should comprise two paragraphs:

   a The first, shorter paragraph will summarise any figures in the table which seem to you to present the problem.

   b The second will suggest ways teachers could make the physical sciences more attractive to girls, keeping to matters over which teachers obviously have some control (for example, they can do little about the advice parents give their daughters).

   The tone of the leaflet is important: you would not want to antagonise your readers by seeming to dictate what they must do.

24 Teenage marriages

Young people in love are not noted for the wisdom of their actions; therefore it is perhaps not surprising that most unwise ceremony, the teenage wedding, remains as popular as ever, despite the obvious and excellent reasons why it ought
5 to be avoided like the plague. Statistical evidence shows quite clearly just how fragile are marriages contracted before the age of twenty-one: more than one in three of them end in divorce. Of course, marital breakdown is a real enough possibility these days for those who wed in their mid-twenties, but
10 youngsters who tie the knot in their teens are playing Russian roulette with three bullets in the gun.

   The causes of this increased likelihood of divorce are also fairly clear. First, although few teenagers care to admit as much, it is generally true that they are less able to plan their
15 futures with enough hard-headedness and realism to reduce the chances of failure to a minimum. It may be infuriating for them to be told that experience counts but surely one lesson experience teaches is that hasty decisions based largely on emotion are nearly always disastrous. Especially where
20 matrimony is concerned, the young often appear to take the view that the dictates of the heart must be obeyed without question, that caution, questioning carefully where one's true self-interest lies and coolly weighing probabilities are not in the spirit of the exercise. Nevertheless, the fact is that marriages
25 undertaken after a great deal of wary, prudent thought are much more likely to last.

   Secondly, the realities of married life frequently come as something of a shock to the young. Mortgages, budgeting, limitations of personal freedom, the changing moods of one's
30 partner, the inevitable disagreements — to say nothing of the blazing rows — and a hundred irritations and complications: the couple may think they are prepared for these unwelcome

actualities, but in the event they do not always have the experience and therefore maturity required to cope with them
35 successfully. 'If we are really in love, we shall get by.' But
sadly it is true that however much love there is, the difficulties and frustrations which are part and parcel of any long-
term relationship do subject marriages to stresses which
youth may not be well equipped to endure.

40 Moreover, any marriage will be especially vulnerable if one
or both of the partners come to reproach themselves with
having foolishly missed out on a period of life whose supposed charms seem particularly attractive when compared
with the apparently duller concerns of wedlock. Ideally,
45 bachelorhood offers many advantages: independence, freedom from weighty responsibilities and financial worries, opportunities to travel, to lead a varied and exciting social life
unburdened by serious ties, to be adventurous in one's career. These benefits are normally denied the married man and
50 woman. There are certainly compensating matrimonial
pleasures and those of the single state may well be greatly
overrated; but there often comes a time in a marriage when
those lost years exert an enormous pull. It may be unsettling
at the age of thirty to think back nostalgically to one's bach-
55 elor days; it is much more than merely unsettling, at twenty,
to pine with bitter self-reproach for what one threw away
untried. Of course, the marriage may weather this particular
storm; nevertheless, what a pity it is not to have experienced
those carefree, irresponsible years!

60 Finally, the human personality never ceases changing and
growing; whether we are sixteen or sixty, the person we are
today will have become a rather different individual in a
year's time. However, the general outline of one's character
is much more clearly defined and permanent by the mid-
65 twenties; thereafter we shall continue to change but seldom
in any very dramatic or unpredictable way. The same does
not apply to the teenager, for whom profound transform-
ations of personality and behaviour may yet be in store. The
young couple whose attitudes, interests and needs were so
70 compatible when they wed may, a few years later, have grown
into two very different people, who, from no fault of their
own, cannot possibly live happily together. 'He is not the
man I married five years ago' — in a sense this is always true,

but when they are the words of a bewildered, miserable girl
75 who can no longer recognise in her husband those qualities
which used to match her own so well, they are especially
tragic.

   Naturally one does not really expect advice based on these
rather obvious facts to carry much weight with the love-lorn
80 young themselves. They will continue to see us as perhaps
well-meaning, perhaps interfering, but certainly as having
missed the point: Love conquers all.

Summary

1 Taking your information only from the passage and in two
   paragraphs totalling no more than 110 words, explain
   clearly the contributions made to the failure of teenage
   marriages by:
   a inexperience.
   b self-reproach.

2 According to the passage, why are the changes which are
   taking place in the personalities of us all, whatever our
   age, especially important where teenage marriages are
   concerned? Use no more than 50 words.

Directed writing

1 A seventeen-year-old friend writes to tell you that he or
   she intends to get married very soon. You do not think
   this is wise, though you have nothing at all against the
   intended partner.
      Taking your arguments from the passage, write a reply to
   this letter, trying, as tactfully as possible, to persuade your
   friend to reconsider the decision. Do not use more than 170
   words, not counting those needed for an address, the date,
   'Dear ...' or the subscription.

2   An article in a popular newspaper begins:

GUIDANCE COUNCILS GIVE THUMBS-DOWN TO TEENAGE
MARRIAGE

Nearly half all teenage marriages end in the divorce
courts. This shock statistic was revealed today in a report
published by the Association of Marriage Guidance Councils. The report argues that youngsters must be made to
see why it is that they are heading for trouble if they rush
to the altar.

The article continues by summarising the reasons the
Association gives for the high failure rate among teenage
marriages.

Complete the article, using no more than 160 additional
words and adopting a style of writing you consider suitable for this type of popular journalism. Take your information from the passage but present it as though it
came from the report referred to in the second sentence of
the article.

25 Unemployment and the not-so-young

The employment prospects facing today's young people are extremely bleak and there is likely to be little improvement in the foreseeable future: the truth is that a considerable number of our school-leavers are never going to find a per-
5 manent job — an appalling situation for the individuals themselves and for our society as a whole. However, we must not underrate the problems faced by the *older* unemployed, problems often rather different from those of their younger counterparts.
10 Generally speaking, of course, the financial hardship that results from unemployment will be greater for those who have acquired over the years a variety of expensive commitments: a house with its mortgage, rates and upkeep, a family and perhaps other dependent relatives, a car, credit repay-
15 ments and so forth. For such people life can be a constant nightmare struggle against mounting debt. Moreover, by the middle years one has usually grown used to a higher standard of living, increased levels of expenditure and comfort based on an income which has steadily risen during one's working
20 life. Very often, therefore, unemployment will mean a change in the quality of life which is more striking and disagreeable the older one is.
However, there are less obvious reasons why the older man or woman may find it particularly difficult to cope with sud-
25 den unemployment. Here we are concerned with certain *attitudes*, which, although they are not restricted to members of an older generation, are by then so ingrained that they are almost impossible to change.
It is an interesting fact that when we ask that most basic
30 of all questions about a person 'What *is* he?' we are normally taken to be asking what job he does. This suggests that in our culture at least we tend to 'define' ourselves in terms of

our work. It is not just that the most important thing we *do* is our job: our job is what we *are*. Small wonder, therefore,
35 given this attitude, that the unemployed frequently speak of 'a loss of personal identity'. If I have no job, then there is no satisfactory answer I can give to the question 'What am I?' — I have become, in a sense, a 'non-person'.

A second attitude — one often openly rejected by the
40 young — is usually referred to as 'the work ethic' and is the belief that one has a moral duty to work, that anyone who chooses not to work is being positively immoral. The view is especially common among older men and women, many of whom, when unemployment is forced upon them, admit to
45 an irrational sense of guilt — in the same way one would feel guilty if forced to steal or lie.

This feeling of shame will, in all probability, be sharpened for the unemployed family man. Although in this day and age, the attitude may be thought to be outdated and indeed
50 'sexist', it is certainly true that many, again especially older, married men greatly prize their role of principal breadwinner. Their self-respect depends largely on their being able to fulfil this role successfully, and they will feel humiliated and inadequate if their families must look to the Department of Social
55 Security or the income of their wives for the necessities of life.

Clearly, ingrained attitudes of this sort will make unemployment a wretched burden, certainly not a welcome opportunity to enjoy increased leisure. In fact, other considerations
60 aside, the offer of unlimited leisure is not one that most men and women would want to accept. Not only is there the problem for those who have spent most of their lives out earning a living of knowing how on earth to pass so many more hours of spare time, but there is in many of us a deep
65 strain of puritan feeling that leisure is only properly earned by work. The weekend is seen as a reward for the five days' work that has gone before; and we deserve our three weeks of annual holiday only because we have worked the rest of the year. Consequently, any pleasure which might otherwise
70 be had from spending more time in the garden, at the sports centre, reading or fishing is marred by the nagging uneasiness that one has done nothing to earn these opportunities and therefore has no right to them.

The conclusion, then, is clear: since the victims of such

75 tormenting attitudes tend to be the not-so-young, it is not only the school-leaver for whom unemployment can be a disaster.

Summary

1 According to the passage, why will the older unemployed probably find it more difficult to cope with a reduced income? Your answer should be no longer than 45 words.
2 In two paragraphs totalling no more than 120 words, explain how *attitudes* contribute to the unhappiness of unemployed men and women, especially when they are members of an older generation. The first, shorter paragraph should make clear why the jobless often experience 'a loss of personal identity'. The second should present the reasons they may feel guilty.

Directed writing

1 A newspaper article entitled 'The Plight of the Unemployed School-Leaver' ends with the sentence: 'For these reasons, reducing unemployment among the young must be our first priority.' Although you may agree with this view, you feel that the special problems of the older jobless were neglected in the article.

   Write a letter for publication in the same newspaper, expressing your opinion and supporting it with material summarised from the passage and presented in a clear, carefully argued way. Use no more than 190 words, not counting those needed for the addresses, the date, 'Dear . . .' and the subscription.
2 Quite understandably, the main speakers in a school debate on unemployment have concentrated on the plight of the young. You feel that more should have been said about the problems of the older jobless so you decide to speak on their behalf when the chairperson invites contributions from the audience.

   Write the speech you would deliver, basing your arguments on material in the passage and presenting your case in a well reasoned, persuasive way. Do not use more than 190 words.

3   A letter from a friend contains the following paragraph:

> Dad says he might be made redundant. He keeps going on about how awful it would be, but I can't really see it would be so terrible. After all, mum's got a reasonably good job, and dad's always saying he'd like more time for his fishing and reading. Anyway, unemployment is much worse for people our age, isn't it?

You feel your friend is being insensitive and write a tactful letter in reply, encouraging a more sympathetic understanding of the reasons a middle-aged man might find unemployment very difficult to cope with. Base your arguments on the material in the passage and use no more than 200 words, not counting those needed for an address, the date, 'Dear . . .' and the subscription.

26 Learning from other people's successes

In 1981 Dr Rupert Sheldrake caused something of a stir in the world of science by voicing a very odd idea which he named 'the hypothesis of formative causation'. Expressed in a general way, the theory hardly sounds sensational: it states
5 that the present behaviour of anything, be it alive or inanimate, is influenced by the way similiar things have behaved in the past — they will tend to repeat earlier patterns of behaviour.

We begin to see how revolutionary Dr Sheldrake's theory
10 is when it is applied to particular cases. 'If animals, say rats, learn a new trick in one place,' he writes, 'then rats of the same breed should subsequently be able to learn the same trick more easily all over the world, even in the absence of any known kind of connection or communication.'
15 Where people are concerned, the hypothesis should mean that the millions of hours youngsters have already spent mastering their home-computers have made it less difficult for today's beginners to learn how to write computer programs and zap space invaders. Or again: the job of learning how to
20 drive, play the guitar, ski, write a best-seller or run a four-minute mile should be a little easier this year than it was last, for no other reason than that the total number of people who have succeeded in doing these things increased during the last twelve months.
25 Of course, the theory, because it involves 'causal connections through both space and time of a kind so far unrecognised by science', met with a good deal of opposition from Dr Sheldrake's colleagues. Obviously Science will be reluctant to revise its ideas of how the world works and admit the
30 existence of a major new force unless it is given some very good reasons for doing so.

Dr Sheldrake concedes that until recently the evidence supporting the hypothesis of formative causation has been 'circumstantial' and inconclusive. Laboratories do report that
35 their rats seem to be finding it easier to solve problems of the sort that require them to learn their way around mazes. And it is generally accepted that new compounds, which are often extremely difficult to crystallise, do indeed form crystals more readily as time goes by. However, Dr Sheldrake clearly
40 needs some controlled experiment to test his hypothesis; only then will the scientific community take him seriously.

It is just such an experiment which he reports in a recent *New Scientist* article. It was conducted in the following way:

Two pictures containing hidden images were devised. They
45 were the kind of patterns of shapes which might make no sense at first but which, after a while, often suddenly reveal a definite meaning; it is then difficult *not* to see the underlying image or to believe that others cannot detect it. Figures 1 and 2 are the pictures Dr Sheldrake used. If, after studying
50 them for a minute or so, you cannot recognise the concealed images, you will find the 'solutions' on page 96. There were three parts to the experiment:

Figure 1   *Figure 2*

Stage one Both pictures were shown to groups of people throughout the world. After sixty seconds, the number of
55 subjects who could interpret correctly what they were seeing was recorded. Precautions had been taken to ensure that subjects did not communicate their answers to each other.

Stage two A few days later, on 31 August 1983, Thames Television co-operated with Dr Sheldrake by screening figure 2
60 during an afternoon programme watched by about two million people. After a short time, the solution was shown and then 'melted' back into the puzzle picture, so that the hidden image was then obvious to the viewers.

Stage three Some days after the broadcast, stage one was re-
65 peated with different groups of similar people worldwide, the experimenters not having been told which of the two figures had been used in the television programme.

If Dr Sheldrake's hypothesis were correct, we would find little difference between the results for figure 1 before and
70 after the broadcast. However, since two million viewers had learned to interpret figure 2 correctly between the two trials, there ought to have been a marked increase in the proportion of subjects who could do likewise.

Ignoring data collected from the British Isles, where sub-
75 jects might have seen or heard about the television transmission, the results were these:

Correct identifications of the two pictures before and after the television broadcast		
	Before	*After*
Number of people tested	754	576
Total identifying fig. 1	43 (5.7%)	40 (6.9%)
Total identifying fig. 2	9 (1.2%)	19 (3.3%)

Whereas the proportion of those identifying figure 1 increased by only 22 per cent — which, statistically speaking, is of no significance — the proportion spotting the image in
80 figure 2 nearly trebled in the second test. The probability of this happening purely by chance is considerably less than 1 in 100.

Dr Sheldrake treats these findings cautiously and certainly does not claim that they prove his hypothesis beyond doubt:

85 'However, the outcome is encouraging enough to make it
seem worth repeating this type of experiment on a larger
scale, which I hope will be possible during 1984.'
   Until now the notion of there being influences of this sort
on our behaviour and ideas has been the stuff of science fic-
90 tion and the supernatural. If Dr Sheldrake's hypothesis of
formative causation is established as 'science fact', the implications will be enormous: all branches of the physical, biological and social sciences will have a great deal of rethinking
to do.

Summary

1   State in a general way the hypothesis of formative caus-
    ation and give the 'circumstantial' evidence which seems
    to support it. Then summarise the implications the theory
    has for human learning. Your answer should be no longer
    than 80 words.
2   In no more than 120 words, describe the way Dr Sheld-
    rake's experiment was conducted and explain how the re-
    sults appear to support his theory.

Directed writing

1   Imagine that Dr Sheldrake's hypothesis becomes an es-
    tablished scientific theory. Write two paragraphs on the
    discovery of formative causation as they might appear in
    some future school textbook.
       In the first, shorter paragraph, state the theory in gen-
    eral terms and summarise the 'circumstantial' evidence
    which supports it. In the second paragraph, describe
    the way the idea was first tested experimentally, showing
    that the results fit the theory. Do not use more than
    190 words in all.
2   Soon after the publication of the *New Scientist* article
    mentioned in the passage, Dr Sheldrake contributes to a
    radio programme which aims to inform the general lis-

tener of recent developments in science. He delivers a talk in two parts:

a He begins by explaining what he means by 'formative causation' and giving the 'circumstantial' evidence which suggested the idea to him. To make clear the importance of his theory, he then outlines very briefly the implications it would have for human learning.

b In the second part of the talk, he describes how he tested his theory experimentally and concludes by showing that the results he obtained do appear to support the theory.

Write the talk in no more than 210 words, adding nothing to the information given in the passage.

Solution to Figure 1

Solution to Figure 2

Acknowledgements

The author wishes to thank Melissa Bridgewater, Elizabeth Ruck and members of the English Department of the Dover Grammar School for Girls for their help and advice in the preparation of this book.

We are grateful to the following for permission to include copyright material:

Associated Book Publishers (UK) Ltd for a slightly adapted extract from pp 84–89 *The Secret Diary of Adrian Mole Aged 13¾* by Sue Townsend (pub Methuen, London); author's agents on behalf of the author, Mary Batten for an adapted version of the article 'Biologists Battle with Killer Bees' from pp 62–63, 90–91 *Science Digest* (Sep 1983); Equal Opportunities Commission for data taken from tables in *Men and Women: a statistical digest*; Granada Publishing Ltd for a slightly adapted extract from pp 102–105 *My Family and Other Animals* by Gerald Durrell (pub Penguin 1959); Mr Ken Hare and the executors of the estate of Peter Sellers for an edited transcript of 'The Trumpet Volunteer' by Ken Hare and Peter Sellers from *The Best of Sellers: Peter Sellers* EMI MRS 5157 (1958); William Heinemann Ltd and Viking Penguin Inc for a slightly adapted extract from pp 65–67 *Of Mice and Men* by John Steinbeck Copyright 1937, renewed © 1965 by John Steinbeck; the author's agents for an extract from pp 100–103 *Looks and Smiles* by Barry Hines © Barry Hines 1981 (pub Penguin 1983); IPC Magazines Ltd for an extract from Rupert Sheldrake's article 'Formative causation: the hypothesis supported' pp 279–280 *New Scientist* no 1381 vol 100 (27.10.83); the author, Laurie Lee and the Hogarth Press for a slightly adapted extract from pp 199–202 *Cider with Rosie* (pub Penguin 1962); the author, Charles Sweeney and Chatto & Windus for a slightly adapted extract from pp 194–196 *The Scurrying Bush* (1970); Thames & Hudson Ltd for a slightly adapted extract from p 34 *Phenomena: A Book of Wonders* by John Michell and Robert J M Rickard (pub Book Club Association 1979); Victorama Ltd for an adapted extract from pp 129–131 *Our Future: Dr Magnus Pyke Predicts* by Dr Magnus Pyke (1980); the author's agents for a slightly adapted extract from pp 9–13 *There is a Happy Land* by Keith Waterhouse (pub Penguin 1964); the author's agents for extracts from pp 180–181, 183–184 *Decline and Fall* by Evelyn Waugh (pub Penguin 1937).

The publishers are grateful to Morgan Sendall at Thames Television for permission to reproduce the illustrations on pp 93 and 96.